Sheriff Joe Arpaio

An American Legend

SHERIFF JOE ARPAIO

An American Legend

FOREWORD BY TED NUGENT

IN SHERIFF JOE'S OWN WORDS
WITH DAVID THOMAS ROBERTS

Sheriff Joe Arpaio: An American Legend

Printed in the United States of America

10 9 8 7 6 5 4 3 2 1

ISBN-13: 978-1-948035-61-3 (Hardcover)
ISBN-13: 978-1-948035-95-8 (Paperback)
ISBN-13: 978-1-948035-65-1 (Ebook)

Published by Defiance Press and Publishing, LLC

Bulk orders of this book may be obtained by contacting Defiance Press and Publishing, LLC.
www.defiancepress.com.

Table of Contents

DEDICATION

For my wife Ava—my best friend of 62 years—and my family, who have both stuck by me throughout my entire life, through good times and bad.

Sheriff Joe and his wife, Ava

FOREWORD

DAMN RIGHT SHERIFF JOE IS AN AMERICAN LEGEND!

BY TED NUGENT

Law and order. Safe streets and neighborhoods. Good over evil. Justice. Accountability. Crime and punishment. You know, radical controversial stuff like that in the embarrassing age of Antifa, MS-13, propaganda ministry fake news traitors, numbnut Democrats, Black Lives Matter crime waves, anarchy, and soulless, treasonous punkass Marxism.

It is worth repeating, ad nauseam and ad infinitum: There will always be sheep and there will always be wolves. And, thank God Almighty, there will also always be sheep dogs ready to take on the gangbangers of society, crushing the wolves and safeguarding the sheep.

My American dream and your American dream are only available and worth jack squat because of ass-kicking, gung-ho sheep dogs like the great Sheriff Joe Arpaio and all the warriors like him on the not-so-mean streets of America.

I'm just a dangerous Detroit guitar player but, first and foremost, I am an American husband, father, brother, grandfather, neighbor, entrepreneur, bandmate, and somewhat of a sheep dog my bad self.

As a sworn Michigan sheriff's deputy since 1984, I have eagerly plunged into the belly of the toxic criminal beast staring down the wolves of engineered recidivism, and understand better than most what these heroes of law enforcement face on a daily basis.

I've studied Joe Arpaio and called him a friend and LEO blood brother for many years, and wish to celebrate this great man's words, deeds, actions, dedication, sacrifices, and commitment dead center in the We The People asset column, making and keeping America Great his entire life.

If real, meaningful education existed in America, there would be a SHERIFF JOE curriculum in every school, teaching all our children exactly where quality of life comes from and how it gets here.

My hero Joe Arpaio embodies the snarl-and-caress ballet of the ultimate sheep dog, proven in his lifetime of law enforcement and the often-delicate balance between diplomacy and hand-to-hand combat tactics.

As fantasy-addled communist traitors among us clamor for reimagined justice, the rest of us simply want pragmatic, common sense law and order where good people are safeguarded and rewarded while lawbreakers are held to effective accountability and adequately punished.

This book should be read, studied, reviewed, and shared by every American to counterpunch the flurry of toxic fake news and communist propaganda that constantly lies about and hates everything Sheriff Joe stands for.

That such rotten people are against Joe is yet more proof as to what a great man he is.

I wish there was already a huge, towering statue of Sheriff Joe in downtown Phoenix and in the town square of Washington, D.C. Such a monument would represent the ultimate celebration of Great America, and it would also represent the ultimate bait for the ultimate scoundrels in their feeble attempts to tear down everything good about America.

Good Americans of every stripe would surround Joe's statues and dare the enemies of America to mess with them, and I guarantee the Joe statues would not be tampered with and would remain standing tall in defiance of the evildoers.

That is exactly what the legend of Sheriff Joe epitomizes—Law and order. Safe streets and neighborhoods. Good over evil. Justice. Accountability. Crime and punishment.

Thank you, Sheriff Joe. We, the People of the United States of America, SALUTE you and thank you for your lifetime of warrior heroism.

Sheriff Arpaio with Ted Nugent

Chapter 1

The Pardon

"Well, a lot of people think it was the right thing to do.... Sheriff Joe, he's done a great job for the people of Arizona. He's very strong on borders, very strong on illegal immigration. He is loved in Arizona. I thought he was treated unbelievably unfairly when they came down with their big decision to go get him right before the election voting started, as you know—and he lost in a fairly close election. He would have won the election but they just hammered him before the election, a very unfair thing to do.... Sheriff Joe is a great veteran of the military, great law enforcement person, someone who has won many, many elections in the state of Arizona.... Sheriff Joe is a patriot. Sheriff Joe loves our country. Sheriff Joe protected our borders. Sheriff Joe was very unfairly treated by the Obama administration, especially right before an election—an election he would have won.... I stand by my pardon of Sheriff Joe and I think the people of Arizona, the people that really know him best, would agree with me.

President Donald J. Trump
White House Press Conference
August 28, 2017

I did not attend President Trump's scheduled rally in late August, 2017 because I didn't want to be a distraction for him, even though I knew it was likely he might mention me.

I've always felt I had a certain connection to President Trump, who was born on the same day as me (Flag Day). We've always seemed to be on the same page and I've always believed we think alike in many ways. Each time I have introduced him at rallies in Arizona and around the country, never once did he ever tell me what to say—or what not to say—which I interpret as trust.

As my wife Ava and I sat at home that night and watched the rally on television, it didn't change either of our opinions of President Trump. While we were watching, I told Ava, "Just wait; I totally understand him. You wait, he is going to say something about a pardon."

I was right.

It took me eighty-four years to finally find my hero, and that hero is President Donald J. Trump.

Approximately half-way through the rally, President Trump began, "By the way, I'm just curious. Do the people in this room like Sheriff Joe?" The question was immediately followed by deafening applause.

"So, was Sheriff Joe convicted for doing his job? That's why. He should have had a jury, but you know what? I'll make a prediction. I think he's going to be just fine, okay?" Trump said to more applause. "But I won't do it tonight, because I don't want to cause any controversy. Is that okay? All right?" the president announced to even louder applause.

Trump continued, "But Sheriff Joe can feel good. The people of Arizona know the deadly and heart-breaking consequences of illegal immigration, the lost lives, the drugs, the gangs, the cartels, the crisis of smuggling and trafficking. MS-13, we're throwing them out so fast; they never got thrown out of anything like this."

Contrary to what many in the media reported then and even now, I never asked President Trump for a pardon. No intermediary ever reached out to me to hint at or discuss a pardon. In fact, President Trump and I have never had a conversation about the pardon, before or since. The only conversations that took place were when White House lawyers contacted me to see if I would accept the pardon.

Several weeks later, I was scheduled to appear before Federal Judge Susan R. Bolton, a Clinton appointee who had found me guilty of a contempt of court misdemeanor (the same charge as for a barking dog), and refused my constitutionally protected right to a trial by jury to fight the bogus charge. During the entire trial, she never looked me in the eyes. She announced her verdict without my presence in her court, and instead released it to the attorneys and media. I knew the deck was stacked.

I believe her intent was to sentence me on a Friday, in front of the media, just so my enemies could see me led away in handcuffs (or worse, in shackles) by a U.S. marshal to a federal prison, with little chance of getting out before the next Monday. Having me do the "perp walk" was exactly what they wanted on camera. I had joked to my attorneys that, at least in a federal prison, I'd get steaks. In my county jails, inmates weren't coddled.

Without a jury, the fix was in, and I knew it.

So did President Trump.

On my wife's birthday, as we were about to go out to dinner to celebrate, I received a call from my attorney stating he had some papers for me to sign and he wanted to come over immediately to get my signature. He didn't mention to me they were the papers to accept the pardon until he arrived. After some convincing by my attorney that these were, in fact, legitimate pardon documents, I signed the papers. After all—I DO have some real-life experience with "fake" documents (Obama's birth certificate). After we signed the papers, we left for dinner.

As Ava and I sat down for dinner at Arrivaderci to celebrate her birthday and the forthcoming pardon at my favorite Italian restaurant in Fountain Hills, my cell phone began blowing up from media from all over the country.

The news was out.

President Trump had issued me an *unconditional* presidential pardon.

While Ava and I celebrated over my favorite Italian dish of linguini and calamari, the White House issued the following statement:

> The White House
> Statement & Releases
> President Trump Pardons Sheriff Joe Arpaio
> August 25, 2017
>
> *Today, President Donald J. Trump granted a Presidential pardon to Joe Arpaio, former Sheriff of Maricopa County, Arizona. Arpaio's life and career, which began at the age of 18 when he enlisted in the military after the outbreak of the Korean War, exemplify selfless public service. After serving in the Army, Arpaio became a police officer in Washington, D.C. and Las Vegas, NV and later served as a Special Agent for*

the Bureau of Narcotics and Dangerous Drugs (BNDD), the forerunner of the Drug Enforcement Administration (DEA). After 25 years of admirable service, Arpaio went on to lead the DEA's branch in Arizona.

In 1992, the problems facing his community pulled Arpaio out of retirement to return to law enforcement. He ran and won a campaign to become Sheriff of Maricopa County. Throughout his time as Sheriff, Arpaio continued his life's work of protecting the public from the scourges of crime and illegal immigration. Sheriff Joe Arpaio is now eighty-five years old, and after more than fifty years of admirable service to our Nation, he is a worthy candidate for a Presidential pardon.

President Trump was excoriated by the fake news media for issuing the pardon. It is my firm belief that this attack on me was orchestrated, not only to defeat me in the election, but because many on the left are more concerned about a certain birth certificate. There are major concerns about what documents, facts, and witness accounts I still have surrounding that issue than on my work in law enforcement to end illegal immigration and my successful jail systems and deterrent strategies such as the Tent City Jails.

Unfortunately, I may own the world's record for legal fees expended on a contempt of court misdemeanor; those fees currently total more than $2.2 million. And, despite the pardon, the legal fights continue, as the Democrats have launched an effort to overturn the pardon. A presidential pardon has never been overturned in U.S. history and is an unfettered constitutional privilege of any U.S. president.

Even today, Federal Judge Susan Bolton refuses to vacate

the conviction and, even though it is only a misdemeanor, we continue to fight in court to have the conviction expunged. But you would never know this was a misdemeanor for violating a court order (more on that in a later chapter) as the fake news media loves to refer to me as a "convicted felon" when no felony charge exists. This has led to several defamation lawsuits that I have filed against the fake news media, which continues to refer to me as a convicted felon.

At 85 years old, and after my 55 years in law enforcement, they should have learned.

Despite the credible threats, attacks, and wrongful lawsuits, I won't give up and I never quit.

Sheriff Arpaio with President Trump

Sheriff Joe greets President Trump from Air Force One

EXECUTIVE GRANT OF CLEMENCY

DONALD J. TRUMP

President of the United States of America

TO ALL TO WHOM THESE PRESENTS SHALL COME, GREETING:

BE IT KNOWN, THAT THIS DAY, I, DONALD J. TRUMP, PRESIDENT OF THE UNITED STATES, PURSUANT TO MY POWERS UNDER ARTICLE II, SECTION 2, CLAUSE 1, OF THE CONSTITUTION, HAVE GRANTED UNTO

JOSEPH M. ARPAIO

A FULL AND UNCONDITIONAL PARDON

FOR HIS CONVICTION of Section 401(3), Title 18, United States Code (Docket No. 2:16-CR-01012-SRB) in the United States District Court for the District of Arizona, of which he was convicted on July 31, 2017, and for which sentencing is currently set for October 5, 2017; and

FOR ANY OTHER OFFENSES under Chapter 21 of Title 18, United States Code that might arise, or be charged, in connection with *Melendres v. Arpaio* (Docket No. 2:07-CV-02513-GMS) in the United States District Court for the District of Arizona.

IN TESTIMONY WHEREOF, I have hereunto signed my name and caused the seal of the Department of Justice to be affixed.

Done at the City of Washington this twenty-fifth day of August, in the year of our Lord two thousand and seventeen and of the Independence of the United States of America the two hundred and forty-second.

DONALD J. TRUMP
PRESIDENT

Chapter 2

My Italian Heritage and The Early Years

I was born in Springfield, Massachusetts on June 14, 1932. My father came over from the old country (Lacedonia, Italy) in 1923. He was an educator and a big proponent of getting a good education. He chose Springfield because other family members had already immigrated to the area. Unlike many immigrants today, my parents worked hard to assimilate into American culture, learned English, and counted America as their home.

Although both of my parents were from Italy originally, and although the families knew each other, my parents met in Springfield. Both of my parents came through Ellis Island. My mother, upon learning that giving birth to me might ultimately result in her death, refused to have an abortion and, unfortunately, died at the age of 23 during childbirth.

She gave her life for me to live.

Upon her death, my father and I moved in with another Italian family and lived with them for three years. Like many immigrants at the time, he became an entrepreneur, opening a grocery store. He added two more grocery locations and a car wash.

My father and I shared a bedroom while we lived with this family. During this time, my father became the president of the Sons of Italy in that region of Massachusetts. We went to Mt. Carmel Catholic Church every Sunday. My father was very pro-Italian and was proud of his heritage, traits he instilled in me at an early age.

Later, we moved in with another Italian family that had three of their own children, until I was 12, when my father remarried. I had a great childhood, playing football, baseball, and basketball; I got recruited by Commerce High School for sports. That is where I learned typing, a skill I still use on an old-school typewriter today. I was a Boy Scout, but only an average "C" student. I worked every day, when I wasn't at school or playing sports, delivering groceries for my father's store. I even picked tobacco for extra money.

I grew up in Boston Red Sox country, so I naturally grew up a Red Sox fan, but we made a trip to Yankee Stadium to see my father's Italian baseball hero, Joe DiMaggio. My father loved the United States and, even though he came here for a better life, he never forgot his heritage.

At 18, after I graduated from high school, I decided to join the Army when the Korean War broke out. My father was somewhat disappointed that I chose to go into the Army instead of attending college and, of course, he worried for my safety if I was to be assigned to fight in Korea.

Before I left for Fort Dix, I got engaged to my girlfriend, with plans to get married when I returned.

The fact that the Korean War broke out did not really factor into my decision to join the Army. I went to Fort Dix in New Jersey for basic training. Once the Army figured out I had a rare skill—knowing how to type—I was held back from the front lines and was attached to medical unit that went to France. This detachment led me to my first experience in law enforcement, as I worked with local French police investigations in trying to combat the diseases associated with French prostitutes. I advanced quickly, becoming a staff sergeant within two years. After the Korean War ended, I stayed in the Army Reserves as a warrant officer in CID (Criminal Investigations Department) for ten years.

I don't remember as a child being attracted to police work, other than the fact that I liked Westerns. As a young boy, I liked to wear a cowboy hat, sheriff's badge, and a belt with two holstered pistols. As I got older, I decided I wanted to become an FBI agent.

When I was discharged in 1953, I took advantage of the GI Bill and went to New York to attend a special Institute of Criminology in Times Square for six months.

I took the test for the federal Border Patrol but didn't pass, but I did pass the test for the D.C. police. My Sicilian fiancé returned my engagement ring and broke off the engagement because I got a job as a Washington, D.C. city cop. She didn't want to move to Washington and she probably wasn't too excited about me having a job as a lowly beat cop.

While I was a beat cop in D.C., I walked the beat considered the most dangerous in America at the time—close to Griffith Stadium near 14th and U Street—every night by myself, carrying a nightstick and a .38 revolver. I was a young white cop walking every night in a high-crime black neighborhood. In my last year on the beat, I was assaulted eighteen times.

In most cases, I was the only law enforcement officer in the area, and the drug dealers and entrenched criminals hated me. Many times, as I made arrests, a mob would show up and nearly turn the arrest into a riot. Badly outnumbered, I waited for backup or the paddy wagon to come pick up my arrests. I didn't have a patrol car. I was never investigated or sued. I even arrested a corrupt police officer who pointed a gun at me. I got this assignment because I asked for it. I didn't care about writing speeding or parking tickets. I wanted action and I got it—every day. Hired at 21 years old, I was one of D.C.'s youngest cops at the time and remained on the D.C. force for four years.

In the police academy, we were taught that, if we pulled our service weapon, we should be ready to use it. There were many times I could have used my gun—and would have been fully justified in doing so—but I used restraint, many times relying on my law enforcement experience when criminals pulled guns on me, and saved many lives when I could have used lethal force.

My first introduction to a U.S. president was during President Dwight Eisenhower's second inaugural parade. As I was directing traffic, the D.C. police chief observed me wearing an American Legion hat with my police uniform. He asked if I knew how to carry a flag. I said yes, and ended up leading the Eisenhower inauguration parade down Pennsylvania Avenue.

Little did I know this event would change the entire trajectory of my law enforcement career, nor did I know I would get to meet many presidents after Eisenhower. During this event, I met Las Vegas Sheriff Leopold, who had come with his impressive horse-mounted posse to participate in the parade. We quickly became friends and he suggested I come to Las Vegas to join law enforcement. Shortly thereafter, I took the Las Vegas Police Department test, resigned from the D.C. police, and four days later was patrolling in Las Vegas. At that time, my claim to fame was that I observed Elvis Presley speeding at more than 100 miles per hour on a motorcycle with a beautiful blonde. I arrested Elvis and took him to the police station, but decided not to book him into jail.

At the time, I also took the test for the Federal Bureau of Narcotics (FBN) and, soon after, was offered a job in Chicago. I had three law enforcement jobs in a year. My highly successful arrest record was a significant contributor to being considered and ultimately hired as a federal agent, even then considered a very fast track to that position. I was assigned to the FBN, which eventually became the Drug Enforcement Administration (DEA). In my opinion, the FBN was the greatest law enforcement agency in history. It was founded in 1930 by the U.S. Department of the Treasury to assume enforcement of the provisions of the Harrison Narcotics Act of 1914. Harry Jacob Anslinger was appointed its first commissioner. The FBN only had 300 agents and a $6 million budget at the time.

I was given a special assignment to the Bureau; it was no accident that I was assigned to investigate the Mafia, due to my Italian heritage. Somehow, the Bureau figured my Italian heritage, combined with my ultra-tough arrest record, would be an asset to the Bureau in mob investigations. I had to interview with the deputy commissioner in Washington, who—in referring to their Mafia investigations—asked me, "Are you okay with locking up

Italians?" I stated, "If they broke the law, no problem at all." I've never had any regard to race or heritage when it comes to enforcing the law. A criminal is a criminal, and it doesn't matter what color, gender, religion, or nationality he or she happens to be.

While I was in Chicago, I was fast-tracked from G7 to G11 to do the job I did in Chicago at the age of 25; this was unheard of then or now. I was very aggressive and it was considered a "battlefield promotion." I moved to Chicago with my new wife Ava, who I met while I was a D.C. beat cop. Ava was a blind date, introduced by a fellow officer. We continued a long-distance relationship during the short period I was in Las Vegas. When I became a federal agent in Chicago, I married Ava and we have been married 62 years.

Interestingly, many of my undercover drug enforcement federal agent investigations actually involved Ava, as I gave drug peddlers my home phone number. Drug dealers would call the house and Ava would play act on the phone as a girlfriend or prostitute so I could maintain my cover.

After four years and countless successful arrests, the agency promoted me to the head of the office in Istanbul, Turkey and parts of the Middle East. Turkey had become a hotbed of opium and heroin, and they wanted me to infiltrate what became an internationally known crime ring that attracted Hollywood producers to make a major movie.

Elvis Presley

Young Joe Arpaio as a U.S. Army soldier

Young Joe Arpaio and his dad

CHAPTER 3

THE FRENCH CONNECTION AND THE BUREAU OF NARCOTICS YEARS

The original French Connection was a scheme through which illegal heroin was smuggled from Turkey to France, ultimately arriving in the United States and Canada. It was likely the largest source of heroin coming into the country at the time. Poor farmers in Turkey could grow opium and sell their crops to dealers at a higher price than any crop they could grow. Opium was a big business in Turkey at the time.

My aggressiveness in arresting criminals was getting noticed in the Bureau, which resulted in a highly unexpected assignment. In 1961 the Bureau asked me to go to Turkey and infiltrate an internationally known drug smuggling ring focused on opium and heroin. Of course, I accepted, as I relished the opportunity to make a dent in the illegal drug smuggling coming into America.

I was only one of two agents to be assigned overseas at the time. I was assigned alone and had to leave my family behind. I took my .38 revolver and they gave me a 1957 Chevrolet to drive while I was in Turkey. I was the head of the bureau office and also worked undercover. By default, I had a diplomatic mission at the same time, as Washington expected me to meet with Turkish officials on a regular basis to update them on my progress.

Despite the fact that I didn't speak the language, the drug busts on Turkish soil got noticed. What began as a six-month assignment quickly became permanent. They wanted me to stay and I agreed, because I never turned down an assignment in my career. They offered to move my family to Turkey but, as was typical with any government agency, it took some time. Even though the Bureau was operating on a tight budget, I was able to convince them to fly my family over the month before my son turned two, which would have caused them to have to pay full fare for my son's seat.

That day in 1962, I was supposed to meet my family when they arrived at the airport in Istanbul. Although I hadn't seen them for five months, I had to call one of the major drug dealers I was working with undercover and tell him I couldn't come that day to Beirut to make the scheduled drug deal. As fate had it, my wife and son's arrival in Istanbul on that date saved my life. The commercial passenger plane I was scheduled to fly on that day crashed in the mountains, killing the crew and every passenger on board.

Twenty-four hours later, after welcoming my wife and son to Turkey, I was on the next day's flight and I could still see the smoldering wreckage and remains from the day before.

Next door to the home the Bureau rented for me and my family lived a U.S. army colonel who was nice enough to let me use his military Jeep, along with my Chevy, to make drug deals in the remote mountains and badlands of Turkey.

My wife and son acclimated to Turkish culture with no problem. Ava even helped me with some of the cases I worked. One example was when I was investigating a Turkish movie actor. Ava and I met him at the Istanbul Hilton Hotel to make a drug deal. During my undercover days, there would be many times Ava would play different roles on the phone to keep my undercover ruse alive.

We were given a poodle by the U.S. ambassador and, later, a Turkish friend presented us with a terrier mix. Our rental agreement on the house did not allow for two pets, so we gave the terrier to a Turkish Consulate employee who gave the dog to a friend who lived sixty miles away. Several months later, that terrier found his way back to our home in the rain on Christmas Eve and scratched on our front door. The terrier, "Tippy," obviously knew my love and appreciation for animals, and that innate desire to protect animals later served me well in a very high-profile animal cruelty case in Arizona when I was the sheriff.

While I was undercover posing as a major drug buyer, I got very good at playing different roles, acting at various times as a French buyer, sometimes as an American, occasionally something else. Here I was, in an extremely dangerous environment with the odds against me again, but I wasn't going to let the Bureau down.

It wasn't so much that I was a great actor; the fact was that the drug dealers were greedy and were only interested in my money. The Turkish authorities were very gracious and helpful, as I did not have the technical authority to arrest anyone in Turkey without the local police. Of course, I had to find local authorities I could trust with my life, which was no easy task.

The closest I came to being killed on duty at that time was in a drug deal in Turkey. In most cases, I was traveling 300 miles plus to meet drug dealers undercover in isolated areas. At any moment, the Turkish authorities could rat me out.

In one drug deal that went wrong, two Turkish suspects were killed in a gun battle. The regional governor charged everyone involved, but I was later cleared. The effort I used to establish relationships with the local police ultimately helped me out, as they vouched for me to high Turkish officials. The many times I shared the food I bought with my own money with Turkish police on stakeouts and drug deals paid off. They would even eat my Spam™.

The U.S. government bankrolled me with just enough money to pay off police and informants, and to be able to flash cash to drug dealers. My high drug busts were getting noticed in the Bureau and around the world. Ironically, I doubt whether the U.S. government would have helped me at all as I didn't have a diplomatic passport to avoid prosecution. The Turks could have made up anything and jailed me but, in the end, they really liked me and what I was doing.

I was never afraid of the risks in Turkey. After I made a drug bust with more than a ton of opium, the largest seizure in the world, I made the local news in Springfield, Massachusetts, my home town, as the local hero and special agent in charge in Turkey. My father, who was so worried about me seeing conflict in the Korean War, now had something new to worry about—whether his son would come home alive from Turkey. When the shooting broke out in that drug bust, I heard the bullets whizzing by my head. About 22 Turkish farmers who brought the opium all came armed. I had a gun put to my head by the dealer; luckily, he never pulled the trigger when the chaos began. I couldn't tell you to this day who shot first, or if any of my shots reached their intended targets.

I traveled over the entire region to arrest drug peddlers, including Syria, the Middle East, Lebanon, and other countries. The groundwork I laid out and the connections I made would later help agencies from three countries (U.S., France, and Turkey) put an end to the French Connection. Ultimately, $70 million worth of heroin seized on arrival in New York was later discovered missing, replaced with flour by some crooked New York City cops. That part of the story was the essence of the movie, *The French Connection,* that was made in the early 1970s. Very little, if any, of the movie plot actually credited the work done undercover by me and the Turkish police that led to the arrest of the crime bosses and dealers involved on three continents.

The D.C. director personally traveled to Turkey to see me at the end of my three-year stint there and attempted to talk me into staying. But Ava was ready to get back to the United States, and I was ready to take another important assignment involving the U.S./Mexican border.

In 1964, the director offered me another promotion, this time to be the special agent in charge for Texas, including the Texas U.S. border. Ava and I moved to San Antonio, Texas to deal with the growing drug trafficking problem involving that area. Eventually, I became the regional director housed in Mexico City, and was responsible for the border from Brownsville, Texas to California—more than 2,000 miles of border. To this day, there is likely not a law enforcement officer with as much experience on the border as me.

Illegal immigration was not the focal point of our enforcement actions; our focus was on drugs. During my tenure in San Antonio, I received several commendations and awards from Air Force Brigadier General Joseph Cappucci for our joint work with the United States Air Force Office of Special Investigations (OSI), related to drug smuggling enforcement.

While Ava and I lived in San Antonio, my daughter was born at Santa Rosa Hospital. San Antonio was a fabulous place to live, and Texas will always hold a special place in our hearts.

I was again promoted in 1968 as special agent in charge to cover D.C., Virginia and Maryland, where I spent eight months before getting another promotion to deputy regional director of the Bureau of Narcotics for the Maryland region, where I personally investigated and arrested a deputy regional director from another drug enforcement agency for selling huge amounts of heroin from his office. That year, I met with President Lyndon B. Johnson and other officials in the White House to strategize drug enforcement at the border.

During the period of 1970 to 1973, I was the regional director for the FBN based in Mexico City, where I moved Ava and the family. I was over Mexico, Central, and South America for the agency. I took the place of a former director who mysteriously drowned in Acapulco. I had offices in Mexico, Panama, and Argentina.

Noriega was famous for playing both sides—playing the law enforcement side with us, yet working with the drug lords throughout Central and South America and France.

While I was in Mexico, I had a diplomatic passport and I spent a lot of time with the Mexican attorney general. My father even came to Mexico and had dinner with us, and was very impressed with the house, the maids, and the attorney general. He wasn't quite as worried about my health as he was when I was in Turkey. During the period he visited us, my father was battling cancer.

The attorney general really liked Ava's blueberry pie and would jump at the chance to have dinner and partake of it. A little whiskey and Ava's blueberry pie went a long way to gaining cooperation with the Mexican government. I got more done with blueberry pie and American whiskey than that big stick.

My career with the agency continued to flourish with a promotion in 1973 to section chief, office of intelligence, U.S. Department of Justice at the newly formed U.S. Drug Enforcement Administration in Washington, D.C., and a promotion to New England DEA deputy regional director in 1974. I remained in Boston until 1978, when I became the special agent in charge of the Arizona region for the DEA, once again covering the border.

Similar to my time in San Antonio, I built incredible relationships with Arizona federal Border Patrol and Immigrations and Customs Enforcement leaders along the border. But I also built relationships with Mexican law enforcement authorities that would be beneficial to me later when I became the sheriff of Maricopa County.

I remained in that role until I eventually retired from the DEA in 1982 after 26 years and have lived in Arizona ever since. Because I thought my law enforcement days were behind me, I started working with Ava in her travel agency business which, at 40 years, is still in business. Little did I know that another significant chapter of my law enforcement career was about to begin.

Special Agent in Charge Joe Arpaio,
U.S. Bureau of Narcotics, making the largest
opium drug bust in the world working undercover in Turkey

Special Agent in Charge Joe Arpaio with the Turkish National Police Chief

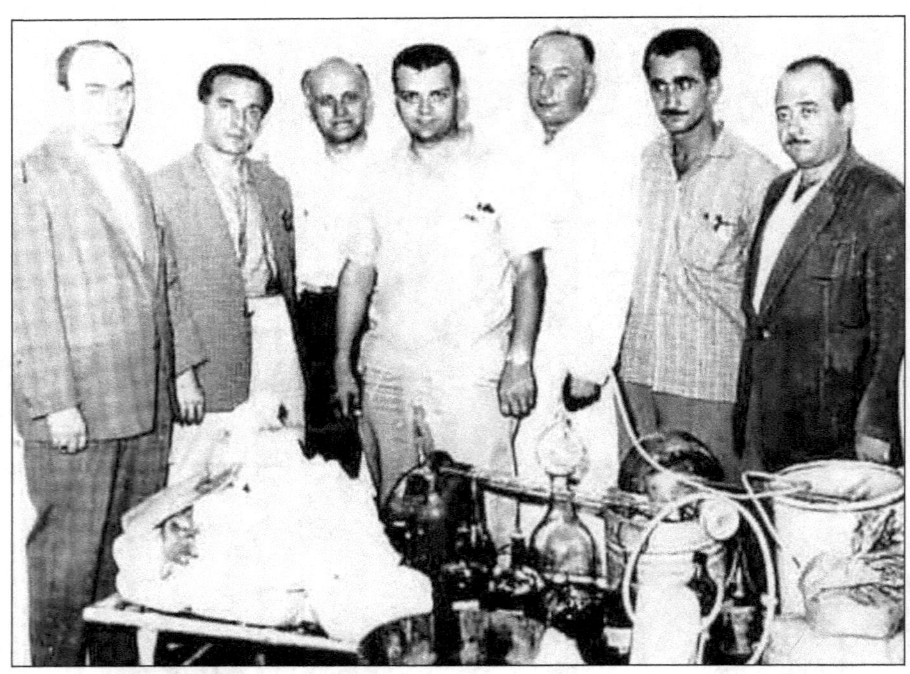

Special Agent in Charge Joe Arpaio makes major drug laboratory bust in Turkey

THE ATTORNEY GENERAL
WASHINGTON

May 15, 1968

Dear Mr. Arpaio:

Associate Director Giordano has informed me of your courageous performance in effecting the arrest of Joseph E. Huber, Jr. and Joseph E. McGough in Vienna, Virginia during the early morning hours of May 11, 1968.

I should like to commend you for the daring manner in which you were able to disarm your assailants. Your coolness and your excellent judgment under desperate conditions are an example for all of your colleagues in law enforcement.

With my best wishes for continued success.

Sincerely,

Ramsey Clark
Attorney General

Mr. Joseph M. Arpaio
Bureau of Narcotics and
Dangerous Drugs
Internal Revenue Service Building
Washington, D. C. 20224

CHAPTER 4

OPERATION INTERCEPT

In the fall of 1969, President Richard Nixon launched an anti-drug war, primarily targeting marijuana being smuggled into the United States from Mexico, and heroin and opium coming from Turkey through the French Connection.

At the tip of the spear for Operation Intercept was White House Assistant G. Gordon Liddy, and me as a deputy regional director of the U.S. Bureau of Narcotics. During a two-week period that fall, Operation Intercept virtually shut down the U.S. border; every person and vehicle that crossed the southern border into the United States was searched.

Mexico, which, up until that time, had never seriously committed Mexican national resources to fight the drug smuggling epidemic, now saw its economy being dismantled as trade with the U.S. ground to a stop. Nixon caused a bilateral reset and bent Mexico to his will to finally engage in the drug war. Nixon did what President Trump is doing with the cartel drug wars and illegal immigration.

Thus began the original deployment of radar and other means to detect illegal entries into the United States at the southern border. Even commercial passenger flights from Mexico coming into the U.S. were impacted.

My work on Operation Intercept is what led me to be assigned in 1970 to Mexico. During this period, I developed a close relationship with U.S. Attorney General Richard Kleindienst. I overheard telephone conversations with Acting FBI Director Patrick Gray, including one very nasty one while I was alone with Kleindienst in a hotel room across from the Watergate Hotel.

Years later, when I was the Maricopa County sheriff, Kleindienst's son actually investigated me when he worked for the U.S. attorney's office in Arizona. Like many others, nothing came of this politically motivated bogus investigation. Ironically, as has happened throughout my career with thin threads and various degrees of separation, G. Gordon Liddy's son was the Maricopa County deputy county attorney who defended me on behalf of the county in the Melendres trial.

Attorney General Kleindienst would come to my aid when I was the regional director for the BNDD covering Mexico, Central and South America, when the U.S. ambassador to Paraguay tried to interfere with my operations. That intervention allowed me to extradite the world's top cartel leader, flying him at night and under cover directly to Dallas to stand trial.

Operation Intercept proved successful, not so much in the actual drug busts that occurred during that controversial two-week period, but because of the message it sent to the smugglers, dealers, and the Mexican government.

I believe I conducted myself as a patriotic American who

believed wholeheartedly in obeying laws and representing our country, just as expected of an undercover agent or someone who had full diplomatic status. I had a rare knack for being able to relate to drug dealers and local beat cops in different countries to gain their confidence. I could also work through very sticky and dangerous situations with heads of state. This is a trait most of us see in President Trump.

It's doubtful that a county sheriff in America exists who has had more experience in the international realm of law enforcement.

Regional Director of U.S. Bureau of Narcotics, Joe Arpaio, receives award from Mexico Attorney General

CHAPTER 5

TENT CITY, USA

When I retired as special agent in charge of the Arizona region for the DEA after twenty-eight years in law enforcement, I never thought I would someday be back. Ava's travel agency business had grown since I became involved, using contacts I had built over the years. One of the contracts I was able to secure for the travel agency was the Maricopa County Sheriff's Office's travel business, which we bid on and won. For many years, we booked all sheriff's office employees' travel.

Thomas Agnos, the sheriff I replaced, decided he was not going to renew our contract because of disagreements we had.

I felt he was not dealing with us fairly, so I vowed I would run against him and beat him…and I did.

Maricopa County, Arizona is no ordinary county in the United States. It is the fourth largest county inland mass at 9,224 square miles and is larger than the states of Rhode Island, Delaware, Connecticut, and New Jersey. Maricopa County's population was a little more than 4.4 million people in the latest government figures taken in 2018, making its population greater than twenty-three states.

After taking over as sheriff, I was stunned at the waste of the taxpayers' money. The county jails were overcrowded and the county board was considering spending $50 million (in 1993 dollars) to build a new jail facility. The jail facility in use, designed to house roughly 3,000 inmates, had swelled beyond 5,000 prisoners. My challenge was to treat prisoners humanely under these conditions, but not bow to the pressure to release inmates before their time was served. Throwing money at the problem, which the county board wanted to do, wasn't the answer.

The initial idea for a Tent City was to erect temporary tents to ease some of the overcrowding, with the intention of housing only 500 male inmates. I had located some surplus military tents, similar to tents I actually stayed in, from the Korean War through a Department of Defense contact I had in Albuquerque, who provided the tents to the county at no cost to taxpayers. The total cost of the Tent City after it reached 100 tents, holding 2,000 inmates, was a fraction of a proposed new jail at only $150,000.

Tent City Jail was arranged into tent rows in "yards" on concrete pads to give them stability. Only convicted criminals were housed in the tents. We eventually built a smaller Tent City for women and one for juveniles. Additionally, we housed illegal aliens who had been sentenced to one year or less for crimes committed in Maricopa County. Few people outside of Phoenix realized the Tent City Jail was right in the downtown district and not in some far-off desert.

Nothing, and I do mean *nothing,* prepared me for the first of many media firestorms that would be initiated by the liberals, illegal immigration proponents, and others over Tent City. Claims of inhumane treatment—forcing inmates to endure stifling heat that could reach more than 110 degrees—were broadcast on numerous local, state, and national media outlets. Very few reporters or news organizations took me up on offers to come visit the Tent City Jail to see it firsthand.

Of course, it was rarely mentioned that inmates could take as many showers per day as they fancied, nor did they cite the very large tubs of rolled towels that were soaked in ice for hours in the worst heat of the day. False reports were circulated that inmates were forced to stay in 124-degree tents and that the cooling fans were turned off on purpose. Huge coolers, and heaters (for cold desert nights), were installed in every tent. The inmates could even requisition up to five blankets each during cold weather.

Over time, some inmates would lose privileges because of bad behavior. For example, inmates were constantly destroying electrical outlets in the tents, so they were removed. Contrary to false reports, electricity was not removed altogether from the tents as ceiling fans, cooling fans, and tent lighting always remained functional.

During the hottest summer months, the sides of tents were rolled up to assist air circulation. But few critics did enough research to realize inmates were not forced to lie in their bunks all day—especially in the heat of the day. The Tent City inmates, in fact, had more freedoms to roam in the yard and to actually come into an air-conditioned cooling facility, with no curfews at any time, unlike inmates who were locked up in traditional jail cells.

It was not my job to make convicted criminals cozy while

they served their time. Jail should be enough of a deterrent that criminals would want to change their ways and vow to never return. Between 1993 and 2018, more than 500,000 inmates passed through Tent City Jail, including such notable celebrities who did time there, such as legendary recording star Glen Campbell, baseball player Mark Grace, basketball player Charles Barkley, boxer Mike Tyson, and rapper DMX.

In more than twenty-three years, with that number of inmates passing through, the Tent City Jails had very few serious incidents. No deaths ever occurred in the tents as a result of violence. In 1996, however, several inmates started a fire that led to several minor injuries of jail staff and several inmates, at which time I personally entered the fray and convinced the inmates to surrender.

Although inmates had more freedom in the tents than a concrete jail cell, it wasn't meant to be a summer camp. Inmates who wanted to buck the system were promptly removed from the tents and placed back into a concrete jail cell. Inmates who destroyed pillows or mattresses lost the privilege of having them.

We never mixed hardcore criminal elements with juveniles or minor offenders, despite what critics claimed. Tent City Jail inmates were convicted and sentenced to one year or less, with convictions ranging from DUI to manslaughter. But the compound was heavily guarded with razor wire, sentinel guards in watchtowers, and more than sixty rotating cameras. Motion detectors captured any movement, and we deployed Maricopa County Sheriff's Office canines mounted with the predecessor to the Mini GoPro™ cameras nearly ten years before the technology was available. The staff called them "Pupperazzi" and the media picked up on it.

The tents were meant to be a starting point for inmates—not a place to end up. I wholeheartedly believe that being convicted and sentenced to jail means you will be required to forfeit creature comforts and everyday luxuries. During one of the many nights I actually stayed in the Tent City Jails myself (I did this voluntarily to prove they were not inhumane), I was asked why I took coffee privileges away from inmates. Coffee is a perk, I told them. It's not my job—nor the taxpayers' responsibility—to furnish inmates with coffee. If you want coffee, don't commit crime! Removing coffee from the inmates saved county taxpayers $200,000 per year.

Cigarettes were another luxury. In addition to the fact that they were dirty, smelled up the tents, were a nightmare to clean up, a fire hazard and a health hazard, it simply was another luxury that had to go. (I also initiated several anti-smoking campaigns in the county and got tough on merchants who sold cigarettes to minors.)

All inmates were expected to contribute, as idle time in incarceration is not healthy—either physically or mentally. Inmates could volunteer for food prep, kitchen crew, or serving, and other jobs around Tent City. They also had opportunities to take continuing education and self-help courses, with life counselors available to them at any time. These inmates produced meals not only for Tent City, but also for all five of the county jails, feeding approximately 8,800 inmates per day. I believe in healthy meals, and we had nutritionists design meals that always had a vegetable, a protein, and a fruit or starch. Critics panned our meals, mostly the bologna sandwiches that were common for lunch.

Inmates were allowed three 30-minute visits per week, and

those who were locked up from areas outside the county received additional visiting time. Inmates were completely partitioned off from visitors and we cut down contraband entering to close to zero. Inmates had access to pay telephones to make collect calls.

The women in Tent City seemed more adaptable to the surroundings initially than the men. Jail staff connected stationary bikes to a power generator that powered their televisions. This way, they could watch TV and get their exercise at the same time.

I always claimed we would make room for anyone in Tent City. The vacancy sign is always lit for criminals. They were not there for vacation. I would not allow pornography in the jail. When they could watch TV, it was generally P- or PG-rated, and were channels like Disney and the History Channel. The ACLU complained loudly about how inhumane Tent City was—no cigarettes, no pornography, no coffee, and no filth on TV. I didn't care. I knew the truth and so did my staff and anyone else who spent time in Tent City or toured it.

We made national news again when I put inmates on the chain gangs, including females. It was the only female chain gang in the history of the United States. I wanted inmates' experience in jail to be developmental for self-respect, faith, work ethic, and character. The chain gangs were volunteer inmate work groups whose members were considered low-risk. Chain gangs were not punishment or hard labor as a form of retribution for a jail violation. I can't tell you how many times ex-inmates walked up to me and thanked me for teaching them a work ethic while in one of our chain gangs. These people have gone on to have productive lives, and are determined never to return to jail.

The liberal news media won't report *those* stories, but their liberal minds exploded when we instituted pink underwear. Here's why we did it.

As inmates were released, they were stealing the white underwear boxers and socks issued to them when they came into jail. We noticed we were losing a couple of thousands of dollars per month replacing these items. Then it spiked to more than $40,000 in losses, and I felt it was time to do something drastic to prevent these taxpayer losses.

I remembered an occasion when someone left one red sock in the jail laundry, with the result that it turned all the whites pink. I thought the inmates might be less inclined to steal pink underwear and socks. Of course, the media blew up, hysterically claiming I was purposely trying to dehumanize the inmates when the reality was I was all about saving our county taxpayers money. If you don't want to wear pink underwear and socks, don't commit a crime in Maricopa County!

Sheriff Joe Arpaio opens Tent City

Inmate movie night at Tent City

Sheriff Joe with inmates of Tent City

America's first female chain gang

Chapter 6

The Posse

When I was a beat cop in Washington, D.C., the department had reserves who had not gone through the police academy. At first, I was somewhat negative about the use of these citizen reserves, but I did understand it. It served many purposes, the least of which was that it got citizens involved in their communities and provided some volunteer, non-compensatory support that would normally be at taxpayer expense.

Whenever the term "posse" comes up, it harkens back to the days when the local sheriff raised a posse of volunteer citizens to catch criminals as a community when the sheriff didn't have those resources. We can all recall the many western movies where a posse was raised after a bank robbery, and it seemed like the whole town volunteered to ride with the sheriff. Those citizens wanted to not only catch the robbers, but also to get their money back. As there was no FDIC insurance in those days, if the stolen money wasn't recovered, the depositors lost their savings.

I looked at the posse as a secret weapon. If the flu struck

the department, for instance, I had back-up resources. The posse members funded their own training, bought their own weapons, and even funded a posse helicopter and other aircraft for surveillance and other operations we were conducting.

Sheriffs have the Constitutional authority to deputize and/or swear in any citizen after certain training to help them fight crime. But the posse members cannot perform actual law enforcement duties—such as arresting people—unless they are working under the DIRECT supervision of the sheriff or a sheriff's deputy. In cases where they are not under the direct supervision of one of these officials, they can provide support for the sheriff and sheriff's deputies, and can be their eyes and ears when necessary.

It is not unusual in the United States for a sheriff to have a local posse for search-and-rescue operations. We had those resources in our posse as well. At least 500 of the posse were trained and ultimately authorized to carry weapons that they purchased themselves. The department, however, furnished the rounds for the weapons and kept a very tight inventory on the rounds that were distributed. The posse members authorized to carry weapons had to account for every single bullet issued to them.

The ACLU complained that we were using the posse to make arrests of illegal aliens and blamed them for racial profiling. We even used them to help identify and arrest prostitutes.

The more I used the posse, the more I appreciated them. I had 3,000 posse members at the peak, easily five times the number of my deputies. Their dedication was as remarkable as the paid sheriff's deputies. I also referred to our "posse and our deputies" when referring to policing activities when talking with the media. The media couldn't get enough of the posse, and the Americana aspect of old western heritage was now coupled with a huge modern-day county sheriff's department. Despite the media's wrongful condemnation of the posse, they actually helped us recruit thousands of volunteers. These incredible volunteers were dedicated and they worked well with our deputies. We had very few, if any, problems between the volunteers and the regular department deputies. The posse was responsible for more than 350 arrests per year and, although they couldn't arrest anyone, they worked very closely with my deputies to put criminals behind bars.

The fact was that our posse became famous worldwide because they were effective. The media tried to perpetuate their made-up lies about the posse being vigilantes, racial profiling for illegal immigration and, of course, the infamous cold case posse that worked on Obama's supposed birth certificate. The current sheriff, bowing to the pro-illegal immigration radicals, has literally dismantled the posse in the county. There has never been, before or since, such an effective volunteer posse as we had in Maricopa County and likely never will be again.

During the peak of school and church mass shootings occurring throughout the country, I decided to train all my qualified posse members in active shooter training. Determined to not have one of these tragic incidents in my county, I authorized posse members to patrol schools and churches daily.

Armed with handguns and rifles, these posse members accepted an assignment with the understanding that they could very well be the first person running toward gunfire in an active shooter situation alone. Waiting for backup in an active shooter situation is not a typical option in order to save lives.

Their courage and commitment to the safety of our children and their community is remarkable as they voluntarily put the safety of the children and the community ahead of their own. On my watch, we did not have an active school or church mass shooting. These volunteers will always have my deepest gratitude and admiration.

Overall, we had twenty-seven different posses with specific purposes, roles, and duties, including a computer posse, an aviation posse, a cold case posse, etc. The posse was my secret weapon and was put together to supplement department resources—at no cost to taxpayers. We calculated the posse saved more than $10 million per year for taxpayers. More important, it sent a message to criminals, illegal aliens, and the drug cartels that we had built a crime-fighting army and, if they planned on committing crimes in Maricopa County, they would pay a price.

I earned the nickname "America's Toughest Sheriff" because I was never soft on crime, built a huge crime-fighting posse, placed criminals in the Tent City Jail with very few conveniences, made them wear pink underwear, and encouraged chain gangs who worked in plain sight as a matter of deterrence.

I had the Constitutional right to swear in citizens for the posse, to train them properly, and to use them under the strict supervision of me or one of my deputy sheriffs. The ACLU and the federal judge later used the opportunity in their wrongful contempt of court prosecution to pull the posse into that quagmire. It was an obvious effort to stop our attempts at curbing illegal immigration, a duty that was granted to me under Section 287g of the Illegal Immigration Reform and Immigration Responsibility Act of 1996. This action allows the director of ICE (Immigration and Customs Enforcement) to enter into local law enforcement agreements to operate under the supervision of ICE for the identification, arrest, and detainment of those with criminal charges and convictions.

The posse was intimately involved in the community. The members of the posse were always willing to give their time and their money to community causes, especially for the Maricopa County Sheriff's Memorial Fund that provided needed financial assistance to the widows and surviving families of officers lost in the line of duty in our county and across the state of Arizona. The posse also volunteered thousands of hours each year at local malls to patrol parking lots and mall premises to keep shoppers safe during the holiday seasons.

The air posse, on average, would rescue fifty hikers, hunters, and lost individuals in the desert and mountains; many times we deployed 250 or more posse volunteers. Their extraordinary heroism in saving countless lives cannot be underestimated. The sheriff's office could never deploy that many resources at once, and were simply determining life or death for stranded individuals by the sheer response time and professional coordination. Many of these individuals owe their lives to the posse.

Perhaps there was no more famous unit in the posse than the cold case posse that became infamous for the investigation into the supposed birth certificate document that became such a lightning rod at the time—and continues to this day. The cold case posse and the professionals who were involved, including me, have been scorned, ridiculed, and publicly denounced as the originators of the so-called "Birther" movement. This unit and its work on the document investigation have had unimaginable consequences and is a stand-alone, political thriller-type story discussed in a later chapter.

We didn't take just anyone into the posse. We did background checks and never let convicted felons join the ranks. We also did psychological evaluations to make sure individuals wanted to volunteer for the right reasons and that they were of stable mind and character. Did we have any bad apples? Sure—in an organization of 3,000 volunteers, it is bound to happen and is no different than any other law enforcement organization in the world.

Our best recruiters for the posse were current posse members, who were excited and willing to share their experiences with posse recruits. We had every diverse minority group and some women included in the posse ranks. There were even posse members who moved to Phoenix simply for the opportunity to join the posse. Our model was soon adopted in various fashions by law enforcement organizations around the country and around the world. Rarely a week went by without the visitation of another sheriff or media member to come and get a real sense of why our posse program was so successful.

Average posse members would spend anywhere from $1,500 to $2,000 or more of their own money for hot and cold weather uniforms, body armor, flashlight, whistle, night stick and, if qualified, the firearm of their choice. They even plunked down $35 for the badge that had "Sheriff's Posse" emblazoned above the star instead of "Deputy Sheriff." The posse was dedicated to the act of "volunteerism" to help us fight crime and, to be honest, they were enamored with my style of tough love, from the Tent City Jails to no coffee or movies for prisoners, the pink underwear, and the chain gangs. They simply wanted to be a part of it.

Posse members could use their talents in the areas they had the most experience, whether it was the lakes' patrol posse, air posse, horseback posse, search and rescue, or whatever they felt passionate about donating their time for. Only about 800 of the 3,000 posse volunteers went through the intensive firearm training and carried a weapon. I would also tell posse recruits that, if I didn't carry a weapon (and I didn't and I don't—for better or worse, despite the threats to my life), they didn't necessarily need to carry a weapon to be effective in the posse.

ABC did a hit piece on my oldest posse member, who was 85 years old and still carried a weapon. The liberal media would do anything possible to portray the posse as incompetent vigilantes with no training who were focused on racial profiling of illegal aliens. Very few news outlets covered the story of me sending a 600-member posse into the crime-infested Van Buren Street area that was rife with drugs and prostitution. It resulted in 150 arrests and the presence of the posse dispersed the criminals that weren't caught like cockroaches in daylight. The media again focused on the meals in Tent City, especially the bologna sandwiches, but ignored the major success the posse was having in fighting street crime.

At one point, the board of supervisors, which sets our budget, removed more than $10 million out of our budget at a time when we were short of deputies and our patrol cars averaged 150,000 miles on their odometers. Had I not come up with the idea of the posse, the good citizens of Maricopa County would have been overrun with crime. Of course, there were some risks. Anytime you place volunteers in law enforcement with less training than the licensed deputies, you risk something bad happening that the liberal left would exploit endlessly. Fortunately, I was willing to take that risk and I was always willing to take the heat for the posse if necessary.

But seriously, what choice did I have? I was elected to fight crime and I'd be damned if I'd let a budget shortfall impact my ability to keep our citizens safe. Obviously, the citizens agreed, re-electing me to six consecutive terms.

Despite the outstanding work done by the posse, the ACLU and other organizations continued to attack the posse as vigilantes, storm troopers, or quasi-militia, which in kind were picked up by liberal news outlets who parroted the same moronic, uneducated drivel.

The posse members have always been extremely proud of their service to the citizens of Maricopa County and the good work they perform at their own risk on a daily basis. Those that are informed are grateful.

In most times, simply throwing money at a problem is no solution at all. Using my substantial experience in recruiting others to join me in fighting crime has been my modus operandi from my time as a beat cop to tracking down drug smugglers in Turkey or cartel members in Mexico. I have always taken my job to enforce the law seriously, and the posse was an answer to the hand I was dealt. I turned it into a winning hand and into a culture that has been duplicated across the world.

After the coordinated and strategic wrongful misdemeanor prosecution and conviction by the forces against me, the sheriff who was elected has steadily dismantled the posse, and crime has risen as a direct correlation.

Sheriff Joe enlists help from citizens to fight illegal immigration

Sheriff Joe Arpaio with his typewriter that he still uses to this day

Joe Arpaio is sworn in for his first term as Maricopa County sheriff

Chapter 7

The Obama Birth Certificate

Throughout my extensive law enforcement career, my absolute stance on enforcing the laws on the books sometimes drew criticism and controversy, but it also vaulted me to advancement with every agency I was associated with. Being "America's Toughest Sheriff" was a moniker I was proud of. Sheriffs from around the country considered me a "national sheriff" and applauded my tactics and strict enforcement of laws; they knew why we used certain law enforcement strategies and the resulting success we were having despite the attacks from the media, Democrats, and the ACLU. Of all the events in my career, from the French Connection, to the pink underwear, the chain gangs, the tent city jails, or the arrests of illegal aliens—none could compare, even remotely, to the controversy over President Obama's birth certificate.

This controversial single issue has changed national politics, resulted in my "kangaroo" contempt of court conviction with an activist and biased federal judge, and exposed the tip of the iceberg in what is now considered a very corrupt Justice Department, FBI, and the national intelligence apparatus. My investigation into the legitimacy of the Obama birth certificate completely altered national politics for both Democrats and Republicans and spawned a backlash the likes of which has never been seen.

Of course, I knew the angst from the Left that would be stirred like a hornet's nest by turning over this rock, but it would have been hard to foresee or estimate the sheer intensity of the opposition to this effort. Nor could I have guessed the depth and breadth of the "Deep State" and the bias of the highly placed officials involved in our federal government, including the intelligence agencies, the FBI, the Justice Department, and even our courts.

Little did I know at the time about the Perkins Coie law firm, which represented the Democratic Party and allegedly hired and paid Fusion GPS to create the infamous, fake, and unverified Steele dossier used in the Russian Hoax later against President Trump. This fake dossier was used to get FISA court warrants to spy on the Trump election campaign.

Perkins Coie has been at the center of almost every political attack against me. They, along with twenty-four Democratic members of the U.S. House of Representatives, led by House Judicial Committee Chairman Jerry Nadler, have appealed to the Ninth Circuit to overturn the pardon I received from President Trump.

Perkins Coie attorney Judith Corley personally flew to Hawaii to pick up the alleged birth certificate from the Hawaii Department of Health and brought it back for a press conference later, but reporters were never able to see the physical document. Some would argue that the reason Obama sent his personal attorney versus the White House counsel kept the document from being archived in official White House records.

Perkins Coie and George Soros supported my opponents in the 2016 sheriff's race to the tune of nearly $3 million to defeat me. This is probably a record for a local sheriff's race. To state that Perkins Coie and their minions were agitated about my success in arresting and deporting illegal aliens and the investigation of the alleged Obama birth certificate may be the understatement of the century.

Let me be crystal clear…the Obama birth certificate forgery, although hidden in plain sight, may be the largest hoax and cover-up scandal in American history.

To connect all the related dots that spread throughout government and politics to this issue would be like reading a spy novel or political thriller. Unfortunately, the names that are tied to this scandal are still in the news today—and they still haunt President Trump. If you saw an organized crime blackboard, with pictures and connected dotted lines on this scandal, it would have the pictures of these notorious characters who, for the most part, have all remained relevant to the hoaxes and notorious, baseless investigations of President Trump. Familiar names like John Brennan, James Clapper, Robert Mueller, Jim Comey, Loretta Lynch, Eric Holder, Samantha Powers, and the Perkins Coie law firm would populate that blackboard. NSA and CIA whistleblower Dennis Montgomery, billionaire Tim Blixseth, Federal Judge G. Murray Snow and, of course, Obama himself would be connected with dotted lines like a giant spider web. The depth and breadth of the criminal activity of the intelligence communities is unlike anything I ever saw in my years of investigating organized crime.

The same intelligence community that chose to attack me has

also directed its attacks at President Trump throughout his presidency, from the spying on his campaign, to the Russia Hoax, to the illegitimate impeachment. The leaks that were perpetrated on my sheriff's office ahead of critical junctures of the birth certificate investigation were perpetrated by the same people who spied on the Trump presidential campaign and continued to leak sensitive information about President Trump's White House in the first months of his presidency. It's now common knowledge that those same corrupt federal cops and cast of characters entrapped General Michael Flynn and others.

The measures that have been taken to demonize anyone associated with our investigation—or anyone else who subscribes to the fact that the certificate presented by the White House is anything but a copy of a genuine birth certificate—would rival any political witch hunt ever perpetrated.

To be honest, an entire book could be written on this subject alone. In fact, a full-blown Congressional investigation and a special prosecutor should have been appointed a very long time ago.

The depth at which this issue encompasses American politics and all three branches of government is not fully comprehended by the public—nor by our elected representatives. There has been a calculated and determined effort to undermine the validity of our investigation at every turn.

Once my investigators began connecting the dots, a tangled web of outright criminal deception that involved many levels of government began to become clearer with each passing day. The issue of the legitimacy of President Obama's birth certificate has been skillfully and dangerously hidden in plain sight. The emperor has no clothes, yet we are the only ones to call it out.

The intensity of the backlash that this investigation ignited still rages today, as the Left assigns anyone who subscribes to the factual evidence that this document is forged as a "birther" and a lunatic, foil-hat conspiracy nutcase. For those who have studied our investigation and results and admit there is ample evidence of a forgery, they also have been lumped in with the crazies who regularly claim to get snatched up by alien beings from outer space and then placed back on earth. And it's not just the mainstream media. Even seasoned journalists and supposedly respected Republicans and other law enforcement branches have purposely shied away from the subject as it if was the bubonic plague.

For them, it's convenient and easy to shrug off the obvious facts about the document and just blame the hysteria on conspiracy theorists and crazy old Joe.

However, there is no mistaking the outrage in today's supercharged politically correct environment. In today's polarized political environment, I could competently argue that it is worse to be accused an alleged "racist" than be a suspected "terrorist." And, of course, any criticism of Obama of any kind *has* to be rooted in some type of racism, doesn't it? After all, Obama was our first half-black president and any question on his constitutional legitimacy is rooted in racism, they claim.

The potential constitutional issues that could be at stake if the facts about the forged birth certificate were really considered and accepted have unimaginable and far-reaching consequences—consequences that few have the stomach or courage to investigate further. The least of these is the validity of any law, treaty, or executive order that may have been signed by Obama as an illegitimate president. It is a question our country has never had to answer in our history.

Coupling the race issue with the invalidation of the first mixed-race president is simply too much to consider or bear for the Left, elitists, and media. The GOP has, for the most part, disavowed what is plainly in front of them, choosing to avoid being lumped in with our ilk, desperate not to be somehow labeled "racist." Democrats retreated hastily and shamefully and still cower in a corner when they are asked if they subscribe to the "birther" theory. Only President Trump, who made mention of this subject consistently on the campaign trail, kept it an open question. I have to believe that all his handlers and advisors since he arrived in the White House have literally begged him to drop the subject and, for the most part, he has. It is my humble opinion that President Trump hasn't changed his mind; he also believes the birth certificate is forged.

For twenty-four years, long-standing Republicans who came to Arizona to campaign would reach out to me for an endorsement to help carry the state or to help them at home. An endorsement from a tough, law-and-order sheriff who was nationally popular was considered a badge of honor, even if their elections didn't include voters in Arizona. The list of those who personally asked for my endorsement is long and includes everyone from John McCain (who later became an enemy) to George W. Bush, Mitt Romney, Rick Perry, Ted Cruz, along with many other presidential candidates and, of course, my hero, President Donald J. Trump.

The steady stream of politicians coming to Arizona to seek

endorsements began to dwindle somewhat, however, as the birth certificate investigation grew in notoriety and length, and with the vicious coordinated attacks that also came from all corners—from the media and both parties. Soon, many in the GOP would quietly and disgracefully disavow me, with the exception of my hero, President Trump, who continued to have me at rallies throughout his campaign. Trump never hesitated for one second while he was on the campaign trail to let the world know the birth certificate was forged.

To understand the full context of how the birth certificate drama unfolded, one must understand that I was elected by the people of Maricopa County to enforce laws and to fight crime. My department was already very heavily involved with official government document fraud cases that were pervasive in the illegal immigration community. Investigating fake documents of official records like birth certificates, drivers' licenses, and social security cards was a regular occurrence for our investigators. Government document fraud is a crime at any level; it's as simple as that.

Contrary to how it has been portrayed in the media, we didn't originate the birth certificate issue. You can thank candidate Hillary Clinton's campaign and supporters for originally bringing up the question during the Democratic presidential primary in 2008.

Then, in 2011, best-selling author, Harvard Ph.D., and respected journalist Dr. Jerome Corsi released a book entitled, "Where's the Birth Certificate?", which raised legitimate questions about President Obama's life history, birthplace, and birth certificate. Until our research, Dr. Corsi was likely the most notable expert on this topic. Today, I would argue my investigator Mike Zullo is the most knowledgeable person on this subject and, in fact, he interviewed Dr. Corsi for 16 hours early in the investigation.

During the first term of the Obama presidency in 2011, major Tea Party groups approached me to request that I investigate the birth certificate issue. In one meeting with county residents, attended by more than two hundred people, they *demanded* we investigate it. While not giving them a definitive answer that night, I thought about it for the next twenty-four hours and decided that, yes, it was my duty, especially if no other law enforcement agency was investigating the situation. After all, President Obama was on the presidential ballot in Maricopa County. If he had been placed on the ballot with the assistance of a potentially fraudulent document, I owed a duty to Maricopa County residents to investigate whether the controversial birth certificate produced was, in fact, original and not forged or doctored. Honestly, I really didn't give much credence to the conjecture that it was fake. I thought this whole issue would die down in a few days after my investigators proved that the document was legitimate.

To be frank, my goal was to exonerate President Obama on this issue and then move on to other important law enforcement tasks at hand.

In November of 2011, I contacted a very capable investigator in my Cold Case Posse named Mike Zullo, a former police officer and detective who had worked closely under my command for twelve years, for a meeting at my office to investigate the Obama birth certificate long form. The long form is supposed to be the original birth certificate as recorded in the county records where a citizen is born. The decision to use the posse was an easy one. The original investigation would use no county funds and would be funded by the posse, which was a 501-c (3) organization whose operations were funded from donations. Zullo had proven to be a very capable investigator. My instructions were to "clear" the president and the birth certificate and to give me evidence if he couldn't. At the time, I didn't feel like the investigation of the birth certificate was in the sheriff's department's best interests, but I also strongly believed that, if my citizens were demanding an investigation into the validity of their elections based on a potentially forged document, I had the obligation to them to do my best.

Ultimately, the decision to conduct this investigation on Obama's birth certificate would reverberate throughout my career in the years after and is still front and center in the national spotlight today in a number of ways.

To this day, I still maintain that I have no opinion on where President Obama was born—and it was not the focus of our investigation to prove or not prove *where* he was born. Our sole mission in this investigation was to determine if, in fact, the birth certificate as portrayed by the White House and the State of Hawaii was an official or a forged document. It was no different than any other document fraud case, with the huge exception that this document just happened to be the sitting president of the United States' supposed birth certificate. I could only imagine the incredible implications if it wasn't authentic.

In the haste to disprove the growing controversy, a poorly forged document was produced and the media ran with it. The media believes the rest of the country is stupid and clueless. A campaign was mounted to discredit any and all experts who weighed in and agreed with the results of our investigation.

Little did we know that this was only the beginning of what we would uncover, nor would I have guessed that the players who made sure the birth certificate investigation was stymied and discredited were at the top of the intelligence community and the FBI. And those people continue to make news today as they construct every coup attempt imaginable to destroy President Trump. These same people are involved with the wrongful prosecution of General Flynn.

My second nature throughout my law enforcement career was to always get to the very bottom of things and let the facts lie where we find them.

To my shock, Zullo came back to me two days later, indicating that the document was a "patchwork quilt" of distinct separate documents laid over each other, and it warranted further investigation. When we announced in a press conference that the investigation was going to be continued, the attacks from the media, Al Sharpton, Maxine Waters, Nancy Pelosi, and many, many others ramped up significantly

How dare we?

Interestingly, we were told, but were never able to verify, that the FBI viewed our press conferences. Surely, they would follow up on our leads, we thought.

Zullo went to work assembling the experts, and we purposely did not include presumed "experts" that had opined on the issue in previous years. Originally, we set a three-month window for the investigation to report back to the citizens of Maricopa

County. Reed Hayes, a Hawaii-based forensic document expert, presented his findings (that confirmed ours) on the document. Hayes isn't your typical right-winged Tea Party type. He is a liberal who voted for Obama, yet he confirmed the document was a forgery.

It's important to note that the investigators were all volunteers as part of the posse. Maricopa County taxpayers were not footing the bill for the investigation and it wasn't until later in the investigation that we assigned a sheriff's office detective, Brian Mackiewicz, at a critical juncture in the investigation.

Our stated goal, even at the original press conference indicating our initial results, was to turn all evidence and investigation results over to Congress and the FBI. We assumed they would take the evidence we assembled and run with it. The media immediately offered a counter expert, hiring a so-called expert with shaky credentials to debunk our early results.

I continued to be amazed by the purposeful non-action of the FBI on the document, especially since the evidence was so overwhelming. Later, we would come to understand why they never seriously considered looking into the document whatsoever—and even went to great lengths to squash and discredit the investigation.

The entire investigation took on a new level with the introduction to an informant who had filed official whistleblower complaints related to the collection of American citizens' personal data by the NSA and CIA.

The famed and supposedly discredited NSA whistleblower, Dennis Montgomery, became the main actor in the unfolding drama of the Obama birth certificate. Montgomery, a self-described computer programming expert, became a partner in the Michael Milken-backed eTreppid Technologies. Originally, eTreppid's major clients were large casinos that developed facial recognition technologies so that casinos could identify blackjack card counters who took millions from casinos while in disguise, going from casino to casino. The firm acquired a $30 million no-bid contract to track terrorist activities for the CIA, eventually becoming the 16th largest defense contractor in 2004. After a dispute over software ownership, Montgomery left eTreppid, partnering with billionaire Tim Blixseth, using Blixseth's political connections to win more government contracts in the same field, under a partnership in Blxware. According to later court documents, Montgomery was once considered "the franchise" and "the emperor on the war on terror" by the CIA. Montgomery supposedly invented technology that could "decode" video messages from Osama Bin Laden that gave signals and instructions to cells around the world, although this was never actually proven.

Blixseth became the connection to our investigation and is the person who originally introduced us to Dennis Montgomery. Blixseth was involved in a highly disputed divorce case and bankruptcy where Blixware's assets, including intellectual properties, were awarded to his wife. Blixseth and Montgomery teamed up to fight the loss of the software.

Blixseth approached investigator Zullo and claimed he could help us with the investigation. Blixseth stated that Montgomery, who supposedly had had Top Secret clearance at one time, allegedly had evidence that my offices were wiretapped, and revealed systemic illegal surveillance on Americans, including presidential candidate Donald J. Trump. In return, Blixseth asked us to help him in his divorce case with wire fraud accusations against his wife. Since those accusations were tied to an alleged federal crime, we couldn't help him, but he still agreed to help us.

Montgomery had direct ties to John Brennan (former White House security advisor under Obama and eventually director of the CIA) and James Clapper, the former director of the NSA, who famously lied to America and Congress, claiming the NSA didn't "wittingly" spy on American citizens. The truth is, they were spying on Americans at unprecedented levels. Montgomery claimed he was the architect who developed the software to "unlock" logins and passwords to cell phones, bank records, email, and credit card accounts of millions of Americans. With Montgomery's program (known as "Prism" in intelligence circles), intelligence agencies had the ability, through a massive government supercomputer assembled in Ft. Washington, Maryland, to do the calculations necessary to apply 10 million password combinations per minute, thus using sheer brute force computing horsepower to unlock citizens' private accounts at will.

This massive supercomputer was known as "The Hammer" and, allegedly, it is still in use today. At the writing of this book, the supercomputer was referred to by General Flynn's highly respected attorney Sidney Powell in a press conference as the possible means by which the intelligence community spied on his phone calls with the Russian ambassador. Used under the guise of collecting foreign intelligence, "The Hammer" was used to spy on Supreme Court Justices John Roberts and Antonin Scalia, FISA court judges, and other political enemies. It's now no secret that President Trump and his campaign believe his phones were tapped in Trump Tower during the campaign, per Montgomery using his software and "The Hammer."

Montgomery's attorney, Larry Klayman, who founded Judicial Watch, filed more than 30 whistleblower complaints surrounding the collection of data on American citizens—all of which went unanswered. Compare that to today, when any whistleblower of the Trump administration is highly favored, and whose identity is masked while Congressional investigations are called. I've never trusted Montgomery—and neither did Zullo, but we knew there was enough truth in his claims to continue to pursue the facts.

I could not figure out how leaks were getting out of the Maricopa County Sheriff's Office so that people were already expecting us to arrive or contact them well ahead of our initial contact. There were only five very tight and trusted members of the sheriff's office that knew our day-to-day operations of the birth certificate investigation, so how could our information be leaked? There's no doubt Montgomery had "some" credible information to allege "The Hammer" was used on my office and my personal cell phone.

In addition to those bombshell claims, Montgomery stated to us that he had collected sensitive information on 153,000 Maricopa County residents on behalf of the NSA, such as recorded telephone calls, emails, bank logins and passwords, and credit card information. Once again, I had a duty to protect my county residents.

Montgomery claimed to have call detail records and recordings of calls to and from the Maricopa County Sheriff's Office, including my cell phone. He even claimed to have banking and credit card records for Federal Judge G. Murray Snow, a George

W. Bush appointee on the federal bench who was overseeing the civil contempt of court case (*Melendres v. Arpaio*) on the arrests of illegal aliens in the county and who eventually turned that case into the famous and corrupt criminal contempt case for which President Trump issued a pardon.

Montgomery also stated that he even had evidence that Judge Snow was communicating with the Department of Justice, the ACLU, the Perkins Coie law firm, and Attorney General Eric Holder on my case. Contrary to what has been reported, we never "investigated" Judge Snow, but we did want to see this evidence. This would become critical later in the criminal contempt of court case.

I initiated a parallel investigation into the potential identity theft of Maricopa County residents. This investigation was erroneously labeled as an investigation into the judge and became known as "The Seattle Investigation" in court records and later by the media, and it was obvious it fueled resentment in Judge Snow that would later come out in trial. Montgomery had claimed the judge's information was just one of thousands of Maricopa County residents. For the Seattle Investigation we did use county funds; however, all funds on the Obama birth certificate investigation were from donated funds.

Montgomery had lost his income in the Blixseth divorce mess, and the government lost trust in him and was not paying him any longer. There were many times, to be perfectly frank, that he would string us along for as long as he could before giving us the information, then only to squeeze more money out of us.

Zullo would frequently contact me, concerned by the

self-described highly erratic computer genius that was Montgomery. Most law enforcement professionals know that paid informants are not always reliable. Montgomery would promise he was "days away" from producing critical information, continuing to make sure his funding continued, but then would never deliver the goods. In my opinion, there were many indicators that Montgomery was potentially a con man, but there was enough truth in the evidence presented to Zullo and my detective Brian Mackiewicz that warranted us to keep paying him. He always promised the next set of deliverables days away, and it always cost the county more money than we expected.

It was also very obvious to us that the NSA and CIA were very interested in what Montgomery produced. There were approximately fifty hard drives of call records with enough sample data for us to know they were real without divulging the entire set of data. Later, we tried to introduce this evidence into the trial in Judge Snow's court, but he would have none of it; he would not allow us to present evidence or even call Montgomery as a witness. He must have known that the evidence would prove he was having ex parte (only one party present) discussions with Holder and the Justice Department on how to frame me, and he wouldn't want that coming out in public testimony.

Meanwhile, as the parallel investigations continued, Zullo and Mackiewicz worked with Montgomery for a year in Seattle, where Montgomery lived. Zullo and Mackiewicz were concerned by what was housed in Montgomery's garage, which was stacked from floor to ceiling with dozens of computer server racks, wires, and processing equipment. Was Montgomery operating a smaller mini-version of "The Hammer" at his home for an illegal hacking operation? He never completely answered that question.

While Edward Snowden is the best-known NSA whistleblower to the public, Snowden couldn't compare to Montgomery in the level of expertise and knowledge Montgomery contained hidden in the bowels of the U.S. intelligence communities. While Snowden was able to successfully disclose and prove the NSA was spying on common American citizens, Montgomery allegedly had the keys to "The Hammer" and was deeply entrenched into "what, when and how" the technology he developed was used. He was always adamant to us that it was "his" technology. What was perilous for the government was that he supposedly knew specifically how the data was used against political enemies.

Case in point: The Supreme Court Obamacare decision shocker wherein Chief Justice John Roberts was the deciding vote. Montgomery claimed "The Hammer" was used to uncover less-than-flattering information on Roberts that was used as leverage to coerce the justice to vote for the administration's stance on the landmark case. Even the staunchest unbelievers on the corruption within the intelligence communities would admit Roberts' vote in that case dumbfounded them, and the only plausible explanation was that somebody had *something* on Roberts.

One thing most people can agree on is the disturbing lack of information on Obama's life. Where are his classmates? Why don't college professors remember him? Why are all of his college transcripts and admissions records missing at Occidental College, Columbia, and Harvard? I would argue Obama has been the least scrutinized president in history.

Why?

In conducting our investigation, the evidence lead to other areas we were obligated to follow up on. For instance, very little media attention was paid to a Selective Service card purported to be Barack Hussein Obama's that was easily and summarily debunked as a forgery.

The Selective Service card lead came to us from Linda Bentley, a reporter at the Sonoran News, an Arizona media outlet. As noted in Dr. Corsi's and Mike Zullo's book, "A Question of Eligibility: A Law Enforcement Investigation into Barack Obama's Birth Certificate and His Eligibility to be President," the copy produced as a result of Corsi's FOIA (Freedom of Information Act) requests show a Selective Service card that was date-stamped completely differently from other cards in the same time period. Filed with the U.S. Post Office, the card has a two-digit date stamp when all others used a four-digit date stamp. Zullo was able to obtain sworn affidavits from several postal service employees who certified that the Post Office only used four-digit stamps in the 1980s for these selective service cards.

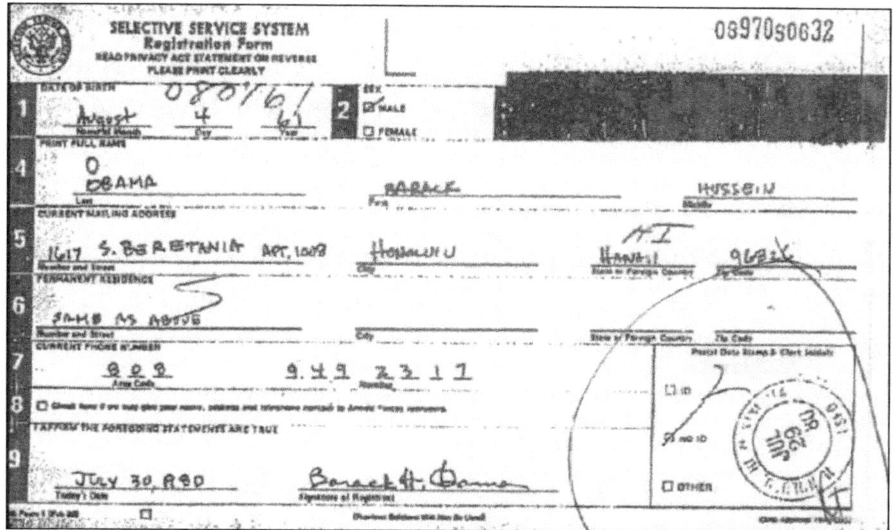
SELECTIVE SERVICE SYSTEM
Registration Form
READ PRIVACY ACT STATEMENT ON REVERSE
PLEASE PRINT CLEARLY

08970s0632

1 DATE OF BIRTH 080761
August 4 61
2 SEX
MALE
FEMALE

4 PRINT FULL NAME
OBAMA BARACK HUSSEIN

5 CURRENT MAILING ADDRESS
1617 S. BERETANIA APT. 1009 Honolulu Hawaii HI

6 PERMANENT RESIDENCE
SAME AS ABOVE

7 CURRENT PHONE NUMBER
808 949 2317

I AFFIRM THE FOREGOING STATEMENTS ARE TRUE

9 JULY 30, 1980 Barack H. Obama

OTHER

Selective Service Card

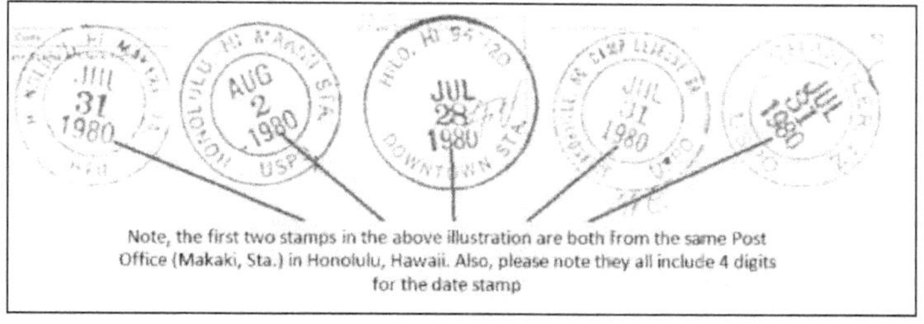

Stamps

The White House refused to even comment on the card, despite the evidence clearly showing it was forged with a poorly-modified hand stamp by the United States Post Office.

In 2008, a federal probe was initiated when security alarms indicated that someone hacked into State Department systems to gain access to a passport used by President Obama while he was in college to travel to Pakistan in 1981. Shortly after alarms were raised, both Hillary Clinton's and John McCain's passport records were also accessed illegally. Many think the later hack of those two candidates in the 2008 presidential race was meant to throw off the investigators' real reason, which was likely to gain access to Obama's passport. If Obama's passport could be accessed and it had a different name, or if it had dual citizenship, for example, from Kenya, or maybe no U.S. citizenship, that could be a key piece of evidence to recreate the missing timelines in Obama's life.

A key witness into the federal probe, a 24-year-old computer employee (Lt. Quarles Harris, Jr.) who worked for Analysis Corp, was fatally shot in the head while he was sitting in a car outside of his church on a Sunday night before a Monday morning deposition. Analysis Corp was headed by the now-infamous John Brennan at the time. They provided intelligence data to various government agencies. Harris' murder has never been solved.

Brennan would later take a "security advisor" role, reporting directly to Obama in the White House, and he eventually became the director of the CIA.

Interestingly enough, Obama never mentioned, in either of his autobiographies, ever traveling to Pakistan, and he even admitted to the fact in a CNN interview with Jake Tapper. Again, the FBI refused to investigate, despite overtures from anyone and everyone that wanted a full investigation. The coordination between the White House and the FBI was clear to us—and to anyone else who looked at the situation objectively. This is the same FBI whose director at the time, Robert Mueller, would become a principal character in the Trump-Russian hoax investigation.

Later, in 2013, Jim Comey became director of the FBI. At that same time, Andrew McCabe and Peter Strzok were also serving at the FBI. To further connect the dots, the corruption at the FBI that began under Obama and affected our forged document investigation would later haunt President Trump as certain Democrats worked to remove a duly-elected president. Obama's administration was littered with stalwarts who could block any attempts to investigate the facts we uncovered. Obama was insulated with the FBI, and had the distinct advantage of Attorney General Eric Holder and National Security Advisor Samantha Power, who were also powerfully connected and could run heavy interference into this type of investigation.

Who were we, some local county sheriff's office, to be investigating their favored son, Barack Hussein Obama?

Nothing, however, could have prepared us for what we found in Hawaii. I authorized travel for Zullo and Detective Mackiewicz to assist them on "official" business for any interaction they might have with State of Hawaii officials. Throughout my law enforcement career, I've been blessed with the instinct to smell danger. This was no different.

It was very clear upon our first visit to the Hawaii Health Department that almost anyone could arrive and ask for a birth certificate with very unsubstantial, even doctored, documentation. Zullo indicated that one person in the department, with no oversight and at that person's sole discretion, could generate a "newly-minted" birth certificate. It's not hard to imagine that, with very little pressure or cajoling, a "new" birth certificate that had never existed previously could be generated. Under Hawaii statutes, Zullo discovered that a newly created birth certificate would, in fact, become the "official" document, even if one had never existed previously under the same name, date, and location.

It's no secret to those in the know that, after becoming a state in 1959, Hawaii would grant a birth certificate to almost anyone to increase census numbers and thus federal money that flowed into the state.

The Hawaii Health Department claimed they had "visually" inspected the original birth certificate, but only released a PDF version of it; they have NEVER produced the original certificate to this day. Experts contend that a PDF document can be easily forged, but noted that a forgery leaves tell-tale signs and clues that it was manipulated. Again, the press swallowed the Hawaii Heath Department's version—hook, line, and sinker.

In the meantime, President Obama purposely never verified or denied that specific document, perfectly maintaining "plausible deniability."

The Hawaii Health Department is required to note an "amended" birth certificate by statute. This notation does not appear on the document.

When they arrived at the state health department offices in Hawaii, Zullo and Mackiewicz were held at security once they announced themselves and indicated the intent of their research as conducting official police business. Next, two Hawaii Police Department officers appeared at the request of the staffer at security who was making them wait as he furiously dialed and made several phone calls in hushed tones so that neither could hear him.

The police officers appeared to be confused as to what the security staffer expected them to do; after all, they weren't breaking any laws. Zullo and Mackiewicz waited in the lobby for nearly ten minutes before a deputy state's attorney general named Jill Nagamine appeared and began to ask them questions about their intent.

Nagamine wanted no part of our investigation, nor did she intend to cooperate. She was very clear that the State of Hawaii had no intent ever to validate the PDF file against the supposed original birth certificate. She was adamant that, under statute, Hawaii had no further duty to validate the certificate any further than the minimum requirements. Unfortunately, using the requirement under that statute, an individual could present bogus documents of any kind and get an "original" birth certificate generated.

She did, however, confirm that the state health department, under no circumstances, made PDF versions of the birth certificate. That document had to be supplied by someone else. But who was it? Creating a fake official government document is a felony, which Zullo and Mackiewicz reminded her of. Nobody wanted to claim ownership of the PDF document, but it was clearly created for this intent. Who could have made it? The White House? A Democratic operative? The FBI?

To be truthful, I doubt the FBI created the PDF version; however, I can't state the same for the other three-letter government agencies. It's hard to imagine that the actual forgery was done by someone highly skilled. The cover-up, however, is a completely different story. Every brick wall that Zullo encountered had the earmarks of intervention from people in very high places. Common practice forensics and document authentication be damned, the State of Hawaii and every conceivable federal law enforcement agency seemed to accept their explanation. The White House distributed images of the PDF document as the original, and the "birther" issue took on a more conspiratorial tone as the media took the bait and ran with it.

The original Hawaii State Department of Health director who "found" the birth certificate and released it was identified as Loretta Fuddy. Two years later, in 2013, during our investigation, Fuddy was on a commuter plane that crash-landed in the ocean near the Hawaiian island of Molokai. All eight passengers and the pilot survived the crash and even managed to don lifejackets and exit the plane before it sank. The entire crash and escape from the plane were recorded by a passenger on his GoPro camera. The passengers appeared calm as they exited the plane, floating in the ocean two hours before being rescued by a Coast Guard helicopter.

Fuddy exited the plane on her own, yet did not survive the crash, although she had no visible injuries. It took two months for her autopsy to be released. The coroner cited her "emotional state" and indicated the cause of death to be a heart arrhythmia, despite her family's claims that she had no heart ailments. That cause of death is almost unheard of in medical examiner annals, as arrhythmia can only be detected in a beating heart and leaves little or no clues in death. The National Transportation Safety Board finally issued its report on the accident in 2017. The report claimed the crash landing was caused by engine failure, but could not determine the cause of the engine failure.

Draw your own conclusions, as with the passport and Lt. Quarles Harris. Apparently, it's not safe to have been exposed to *any* of the so-called original documents associated with Obama's life prior to his becoming president.

Supposedly, a news reporter named Savannah Guthrie is the

only reporter to ever hold the original birth certificate and took an obscure picture of it with a low-resolution megapixel camera. She claims to have felt the "raised" Hawaii seal on the document. She had no idea of what constituted a forged document. Anyone can affix a seal after the fact. For the same reason, a layperson would have no idea if they were holding a carefully manufactured counterfeit twenty-dollar bill. Zullo immediately questioned her role as a "document expert," since she indicated that a 3-D seal was on the document, which is impossible for a PDF printed document. No seal on the original means it's not original. Anyone with thirty minutes' experience in Adobe Photoshop, Google images, and a scanner could create the type of image Guthrie reported having held, and it would still be equally fraudulent, despite where on the document a seal may have been added later. Yet, this was purposely distributed to national media as fact.

Experts can break a PDF document down into layers. If a document has been altered, experts can tell whether font types match exactly, whether dot patterns are the same, whether registration, kerning, and paper patterns are the same we can leave to debate. My investigation led to a different type of analysis, where these issues were not relevant. Again, the PDF document was lacking certain attention to details, but there was enough evidence of forgery to proceed. After much effort, our experts (including others not associated with our investigation) concluded that there were significant cut-and-paste layers in the document. Even pencil marks were visible when the layers were lifted. The level to which the document was forged was remarkable in its implications.

The American public was forcibly fed a massive stream of misrepresentations. Innuendos backed up with sheer media blunt force by the White House, Department of Justice, the Democratic Party, and the complicit media changed the complete narrative. It even became persona non grata for the GOP or even Fox News to report on the story and the results of my investigation. Case in point, when I appeared on the Justice with Judge Jeannine Show on Fox News during the senate campaign, she dismissed any mention of the forged birth certificate, shutting down that part of the interview, claiming the case was closed as the birth certificate had been produced and was, in fact, real.

To fully understand this story, it is important to understand the breadth of the cover-up.

- Early in 2011, Hawaii Health Director Fukino stated publicly that she and Registrar of Vital Statistics Onaka had verified the existence of Obama's birth certificate in a "bound" volume in the vault at the Hawaii Department of Health. However, to this date, Onaka claims he never actually saw it.

- Governor Abercrombie, while running for that office as a congressman, declared he would get to the bottom of the controversy. He announced shortly after taking office that he could not find the Obama birth certificate, directly contradicting Fukino.

- The copies produced for media consumption would have required Fukino to remove the certificate from the bound volume. How did that occur, and why didn't the image reflect that it would have been bound on one side?

- The bound volume would have had roughly 500 birth certificates for the period in question, yet the bound volume has never been produced showing the location where the original would have been in the bound catalogue.
- Zullo was limited by jurisdictional issues to subpoena documents. It would be up to a federal law enforcement agency—minus any interest by the State of Hawaii—to intervene; none ever did.
- Despite the controversy, there are zero claims from other health department employees that they personally saw the original document.
- Governor Abercrombie admitted on a national radio show (Mike Evans) on January 20, 2011 that there was no Obama birth record in State of Hawaii files.
- Less than 24 hours later, Abercrombie recanted and claimed they found a half-written, half-typed Obama birth certificate in state archives. Somebody obviously got to the governor.
- Per Abercrombie's claim, how could such a primitive document (half-written) contradict the PDF document that was produced? What are the odds, out of all the bound records, that Obama's certificate does not have an official seal and the seal did not have raised letters?
- The State of Hawaii has never made the actual "original" available for inspection by any media or forensic experts of any kind.

- The PDF birth certificate document has nine obvious points of forgery, backed by the independent investigation of two document forensics labs in the United States and Italy. These include:
    - Hand-stamped document numbering sequence that aligns exactly with the birth certificate of another Honolulu-born individual named Johanna Ah'Nee (certificate number 09945) who was born 19 days later than Obama, yet whose number sequencing is ahead of the supposed Obama (certificate number 10641) birth certificate long form.
    - Hand-affixed date stamps that have the exact same angle, which statistically is almost impossible.
    - Exact cut-and-paste alignment from Ah'Nee's certificate to the Obama version in multiple locations and not aligned with the line continuation commonly seen on a manual typewriter, which was used to populate the certificates in 1961. It's very obvious, even to the casual observer, that Ah'Nee's birth certificate was used as a source document.
    - Handwritten pencil codes that, when compared to the codes used at the time, would indicate blank fields in origin, but were later added.
    - See these 9 items of forgery at: https://www.youtube.com/watch?v=HZm-lr9d5Po
    - The State of Hawaii has *never* produced an Obama original birth certificate document.

One can only surmise the reasons for a falsified birth certificate:

A. It never existed to begin with.

B. Information on a real certificate is being hidden on purpose, e.g., if parental lineage or place of birth is an issue.

FILE NUMBER 151 61 09945

Child's First Name (Type or print): JOHANNA | 1b. Middle Name: SOLANGE SIERRA OK-HEE | 1c. Last Name: AH'NEE

Sex: Female | 3. This Birth: Single [X] Twin [ ] Triplet [ ] | 4. If Twin or Triplet, Was Child Born: 1st [ ] 2nd [ ] 3rd [ ] | 5a. Birth Date: Month August, Day 23, Year 1961 | 5b. Hour 12:37 A.M.

Place of Birth: City, Town or Rural Location: Honolulu | 6b. Island: Oahu

Name of Hospital or Institution (If not in hospital or institution, give street address): Kapiolani Maternity & Gynecological Hospital | 6. Is Place of Birth Inside City or Town Limits? If no, give judicial district. Yes [X] No [ ]

Usual Residence of Mother: City, Town or Rural Location: Honolulu | 7b. Island: Oahu | County and State or Foreign Country: Honolulu, Hawaii

Street Address: 623 A Kunawai Lane | 7e. Is Residence Inside City or Town Limits? If no, give judicial district. Yes [X] No [ ]

Mother's Mailing Address: | 7g. Is Residence on a Farm or Plantation? Yes [ ] No [X]

Full Name of Father: JAMES KAOHU AH'NEE | 9. Race of Father: Hawn-Caucasian-Chinese

Age of Father: 29 | 11. Birthplace (Island, State or Foreign Country): Honolulu, Oahu | 12a. Usual Occupation: Chief Reefer | 12b. Kind of Business or Industry: Steamship Company

Full Maiden Name of Mother: THERESA PUUKAWA SNIFFEN | 14. Race of Mother: Hawn-Caucasian-Korean

Age of Mother: 36 | 16. Birthplace (Island, State or Foreign Country): Honolulu, Oahu | 17a. Type of Occupation Outside Home During Pregnancy: None | 17b. Date Last Worked:

I certify that the above stated information is true and correct to the best of my knowledge. | 18a. Signature of Parent or Other Informant: [signature] | Parent [ ] Other [ ] | 18b. Date of Signature: 8-23-61

I hereby certify that this child was born alive on the date and hour stated above. | 19a. Signature of Attendant: [signature] | M.D. [✓] D.O. [ ] Midwife [ ] Other [ ] | 19b. Date of Signature: 8-24-61

Date Accepted by Local Reg.: AUG 24 1961 | 21. Signature of Local Registrar: [signature] | 22. Date Accepted by Reg. General: AUG 24 1961

Evidence for Delayed Filing or Alteration

Ah'Nee Birth Certificate

STATE OF HAWAII

CERTIFICATE OF LIVE BIRTH

DEPARTMENT OF HEALTH

FILE NUMBER 151 61 10641

1a. Child's First Name (Type or print)	1b. Middle Name	1c. Last Name
BARACK	HUSSEIN	OBAMA, II

2. Sex: Male
3. This Birth: Single [X] Twin [ ] Triplet [ ]
4. If Twin or Triplet, Was Child Born: 1st [ ] 2nd [ ] 3rd [ ]
5a. Birth Date: Month August, Day 4, Year 1961
5b. Hour: 7:24 P.M.
6a. Place of Birth: City, Town or Rural Location: Honolulu
6b. Island: Oahu
6c. Name of Hospital or Institution (If not in hospital or institution, give street address): Kapiolani Maternity & Gynecological Hospital
6d. Is Place of Birth Inside City or Town Limits? If no, give judicial district: Yes [X] No [ ]
7a. Usual Residence of Mother: City, Town or Rural Location: Honolulu
7b. Island: Oahu
7c. County and State or Foreign Country: Honolulu, Hawaii
7d. Street Address: 6085 Kalanianaole Highway
7e. Is Residence Inside City or Town Limits? If no, give judicial district: Yes [X] No [ ]
7f. Mother's Mailing Address:
7g. Is Residence on a Farm or Plantation? Yes [ ] No [X]
8. Full Name of Father: BARACK HUSSEIN OBAMA
9. Race of Father: African
10. Age of Father: 25
11. Birthplace (Island, State or Foreign Country): Kenya, East Africa
12a. Usual Occupation: Student
12b. Kind of Business or Industry: University
13. Full Maiden Name of Mother: STANLEY ANN DUNHAM
14. Race of Mother: Caucasian
15. Age of Mother: 18
16. Birthplace (Island, State or Foreign Country): Wichita, Kansas
17a. Type of Occupation Outside Home During Pregnancy: None
17b. Date Last Worked:

I certify that the above stated information is true and correct to the best of my knowledge.
18a. Signature of Parent or Other Informant: Stanley Ann Dunham Obama — Parent [X] Other [ ]
18b. Date of Signature: 8-7-61

I hereby certify that this child was born alive on the date and hour stated above.
19a. Signature of Attendant: David A Sinclair — M.D. [X] D.O. [ ] Midwife [ ] Other [ ]
19b. Date of Signature: 8-8-61

20. Date Accepted by Local Reg.: AUG - 8 1961
21. Signature of Local Registrar: UKLee
22. Date Accepted by Reg. General: AUG - 8 1961
23. Evidence for Delayed Filing or Alteration:

APR 25 2011

I CERTIFY THIS IS A TRUE COPY OR ABSTRACT OF THE RECORD ON FILE IN THE HAWAII STATE DEPARTMENT OF HEALTH

Alvin T. Onaka, Ph.D.
STATE REGISTRAR

Alleged Obama Birth Certificate

How does one go through life—even the simple things like playing little league baseball, registering for school or getting a driver's license—without a birth certificate?

To add smoke to an already plausible investigation result is the pattern established with other Obama vital records. Obama's college admission records, transcripts, and papers are sealed and locked down at Columbia University, Harvard University, and Occidental College. It's entirely plausible that they no longer exist. This adds to the theories of whether Obama applied for admission as a foreign student. He's his own worst enemy at putting conspiracy theories to rest. A defense contractor in Afghanistan made FOIA (Freedom of Information Act) requests for Obama's Selective Service records. The requests were fulfilled after a long and protracted battle, but the contractor somehow got two sets with differing information.

For five years, we researched these birth certificate documents, with my investigator running headlong into brick walls at every turn. These impediments weren't facts that countered the evidence they gathered, but instead were delays, brush-offs, and outward hostility by those who should have been investigating after the evidence was presented.

Part of this extensive length of time was the time spent contacting more than 212 forensic document experts; 100% turned us down. "Too hot to touch" or "it would ruin our business" were two common excuses we got from these experts.

We ended up using two independent expert digital forensic document firms, one in the United States and one in Italy. They all arrived independently at the same conclusions. The Italian firm was the same firm that issued its findings on the famous Shroud of Turin—so they were hardly amateurs in this field.

As previously mentioned, even forensic document expert, Obama supporter and Reed Hayes, agreed with our assessment of the document.

I never imagined the level of viciousness and hatred against me and my department that ensued simply by following the dictates of the good people of Maricopa County, who asked my department to look into it.

In his comprehensive book on the subject, Corsi goes on to state, "No federal or state government agency or institution vetted Obama's requirements for office before he became a candidate for the presidency, during his campaign or subsequently."

By 2016, Zullo was able to obtain the Italian forensics results and claimed their findings were conclusive, irrefutable, and unanimous. The Obama birth certificate was a forged document.

Even the press conferences we held at various stages of the investigation were acrimonious, with reporters who were Obama supporters who lost their journalistic qualities and became extremely combative with us when presented with the facts. President Trump could have watched these press conferences to get a glimpse of what he was in for after he won the White House. All journalistic integrity flies out the window when the mainstream media is presented with facts they don't like. We watched news coverage of the pressers later and wondered if the reporters had attended the same press conference we conducted, as words were twisted, quotes were taken out of context, and an abundance of outright lies were broadcast.

Ironically, the entire birther nomenclature was originally introduced by Hillary Clinton, who skirted the issue on its fringes, hoping the media would pick up on it and create doubt about Barack Obama, her primary opponent for the Democratic presidential nomination.

After Obama won the nomination, the Obama team turned the birther tables on Senator John McCain, questioning his eligibility to run because he was born in the Panama Canal region while his father was in the military. Sometimes a good defense is a dastardly offense.

The cloud of Obama's eligibility to run for president was always in the background because his life before becoming a state senator in Illinois was always clouded in secrecy. Those questions dogged my constituents, many who felt the birth certificate was obviously worth an investigation.

The counter-attack from Obama's minions was swift and effective. A public relations campaign to discredit me and my department has been in full swing since 2011. And, despite the outcries about my dedication to lock up criminals with no frills or conveniences, the Tent City Jail, the pink underwear, the chain gangs, or the successful campaign to arrest illegal aliens—none of those issues combined met the level of fury aimed at me for Zullo's incredible job of exposing the truth.

There is no doubt that this hostility and orchestrated smear campaigns led to the legal problems I faced from incompetent, corrupt, and extremely biased judges who were aligned with very powerful enemies from La Raza to the ACLU to the Democratic Party and even some establishment members of the GOP. I've had friends for years in law enforcement, sports team owners, donors and politicians who, like Judas, found it easier to deny their association with me than to look at the simple and obvious facts of the birth certificate.

To this day, while running for re-election to an unprecedented seventh term as Maricopa County sheriff, the issues the Left will raise are not about the uptick in crime from my Democratic successor, the ballooning budget, the failure of the jail system, or other local crime matters. The issue at the heart of my current re-election for sheriff is that I was responsible for proving the birth certificate President Obama presented as proof to the world, a computer-generated image of his citizenship, is a completely forged document.

My investigators spent 15,000 hours investigating this issue. Zullo himself went without pay for long periods of time during this investigation and has suffered the same incredulous character assassination I have. He has also endured death threats, innuendos, and public scorn, but his dedication to find the truth never wavered.

Imagine the ramifications and the irony of it all.

After all my hard work and dedication to enforcing illegal immigration laws, America could have possibly elected a naturalized citizen, born of a U.S. citizen, but constitutionally unqualified to serve as president, to two terms as commander-in-chief and, for too many, it's just too much to bear.

With all that is coming out now, in relation to the government's intelligence coup d'état, the only hope that history gets this right in the near term is an unfettered President Donald J.

Trump in a second term. If not, history may not tell the real story for 50 years—if ever.

Even after all of this evidence that has been produced, Obama was elected president of the United States with not one real vital statistic document that ordinary citizens have to produce at various times throughout their lives.

Chapter 8

Senator John McCain & Vice President Joe Biden

My relationship with Senator John McCain was certainly a love/hate relationship over the years. Despite any disagreements I may have had with him over policies, politics or issues, he should always be remembered for his service to his country.

Simply put, Senator McCain could be very vindictive and hold a grudge for a very long time. Up and until the time that I endorsed George W. Bush for president for the 2000 election, Senator McCain was supportive and always asked me for my endorsement in his campaigns. I then became Bush's honorary chairman for Arizona, traveling with him on campaign stops in the state, much like I did for future President Trump.

To say Senator McCain was not happy with me over Bush's endorsement would be an understatement. He even went so far as to purposely avoid shaking my hand at Bush's visit to Phoenix, despite some very nice compliments and public praise that President Bush gave me on the visit.

Senator McCain worked very hard to gain my endorsement over Romney; however, in the end I endorsed Romney—which incensed McCain.

When candidate Trump arrived for the first time in Phoenix during his presidential campaign, I was one of the few elected officials who stood with him early in Arizona. Senator John McCain was nowhere to be found and proved later to be an enemy of President Trump.

McCain's wife and their television celebrity daughter have never been my supporters and, of course, they don't support President Trump.

In McCain's book that he wrote before he passed, he made sure to attack me for my immigration arrests and other tough measures I took to combat crime. He also took the opportunity to blast President Trump for my pardon on national TV and purposely called me a "convicted felon" in his book when he knew that wasn't a fact. This is the type of vindictive personality of John McCain that I experienced. Below is Senator John McCain's letter endorsing me for "Sheriff of the Year" while I was still in his good graces politically.

Obama and Biden began investigating me 100 days after they took office. Former Vice President Joe Biden also criticized President Trump's issuance of my pardon in 2009. Vice President Biden had a photo taken with me. President Obama also previously had a photo taken with me in 2009 while they were investigating me during the swine flu epidemic, when concerns were heightened over the spread of this disease from illegal immigration. At the time, I was about the only elected official raising this concern.

/08/97 13:58

Senator John McCain

WASHINGTON, D.C. 20510

January 8, 1997

National Sheriffs' Association
1450 Duke Street
Alexandria, Virginia 22314-3490

To Whom it May Concern:

I am pleased to offer my strongest recommendation on behalf of Sheriff Joe Arpaio for the Ferris E. Lucas Award for Sheriff of the Year.

As Sheriff of Maricopa County, the most heavily populated county in Arizona, Joe's creative and aggressive approach to fighting crime has earned him the support of the community as well as lawmakers throughout the state. Joe is well known for his get tough philosophy with inmates. He firmly believes that jail should be a deterrent to crime, and operates the jail system accordingly. Inmates are expected to work hard, TV is restricted, smoking is prohibited and the food service in Maricopa County jails meets nutritional standards but costs less than any large jail system in the country.

In fighting crime, Sheriff Arpaio has implemented a unique and innovative volunteer posse program to build a strong partnership between private citizens, local businesses and law enforcement authorities. The volunteer posses combat prostitution and graffiti, patrol shopping malls during the holiday season, and even round up deadbeat parents. The program is extremely popular and successful in deterring crime in Maricopa County.

Sheriff Arpaio is the toughest, most effective law enforcement official I know. He is hard working, dedicated and has fulfilled the duties of his office with honesty and integrity. He is deeply committed to serving the community, and his efforts to deter and combat crime have been notable.

I am proud to offer my strongest recommendation on Sheriff Arpaio's behalf. I hope that he will receive every consideration. Thank you for your attention to my views.

Sincerely,

John McCain

John McCain
United States Senator

JM/xnj

A copy of the Biden photo was never delivered to me—or was it conveniently "lost"? Is it because Biden did not remember the Obama administration was investigating me in 2009?

Around 1983, I appeared before then-Senator Biden, at his request, while he was the chairman of the International Narcotics Control Hearing. Later, Biden had nice words to say about me and my testimony.

Senator Bernie Sanders made a veiled threat to me in 2016, stating, "If I am elected president, the president of the United States does have power. So watch out, Joe."

McCain also told me he was sorry I lost the 2016 sheriff's race, then he went on national TV blasting me again for my immigration policies and my pardon from President Trump. In his final years, McCain became increasingly disappointing to many, holding up legislation to spite President Trump. He may have been intricately involved with the hoax against President Trump involving the Steele Dossier, the FISA courts, and the intelligence agencies. He also may have had ties to George Soros and the law firm Perkins Coie, which seemed to be a common denominator in all the efforts to destroy me...and President Trump.

During one of my recent national TV interviews, I was asked if Senator McCain was my hero. I replied to them I never had a hero, and it took me 75 years to find one, but it certainly wasn't John McCain...it was President Donald J. Trump!

Chapter 9

The Green Acres 23

As an animal lover, I've always been interested in enforcing animal cruelty laws. My department had one of the largest and most successful animal cruelty teams in the country, with six full-time investigators. During my 24 years as the Maricopa County sheriff, I received numerous awards for my work in protecting animals, including the Humanitarian Award from the Maricopa Humane Club, the Special Community Award from Horses Help, the Lifetime Achievement Award from In Defense of Animals, and a formal thanks from the Arizona Humane Society. Throughout my career, I have always actively sought to protect animals who can't protect themselves.

There were times when we rescued animals and actually placed them in our air-conditioned jails to await adoption, allowing appreciative qualified inmates to care for them until adoption. It was good for the inmates and good for the rescued animals.

We prosecuted hundreds of abuse and neglect cases, including several bestiality sex ring undercover investigations operating on Craigslist in the county that resulted in numerous arrests. We never lost a case, but I was sometimes shocked at the people involved, including some with professional occupations. The successful arrests, prosecutions, and ultimate convictions of the abusers of animals, I believe, prevents these criminals from graduating to other crimes. It's a known fact that many animal abusers go on to be pedophiles and even serial killers.

But few cases were as heart-wrenching as the 2014 case of what became widely known as The Green Acres 23. The magnitude of the investigation and the animal loss was so significant that, as soon as I became aware of the scope and size of the loss of these family pets, I actually went to the site of the crime myself as my investigators were gathering evidence. I had no idea at the time that it involved the family of then-sitting Arizona U.S. Senator Jeff Flake.

My office received complaints from several dog owners who horrifically lost their pets in the Gilbert, Arizona boarding kennel. These owners believed animal cruelty charges were warranted for the neglect and unexplained, contradictory statements made by a young couple managing the business and by the owners of the kennel. It is unimaginable that pet owners could entrust their family pets to a boarding kennel, only to tragically discover that the simple act of placing their family pet in the trust of a boarding kennel would be the animal's death sentence, but that is exactly what happened.

Senator Flake's young adult son, Austin, and his wife were left to care for twenty-nine dogs that were being boarded at a home owned by Austin Flake's in-laws, MaLeisa and Todd Hughes, as they left to go on vacation in Florida. The twenty-nine dogs were inexplicably kept in what amounted to a portable building or shed that was only 9x12 feet, added onto the main residence. The dog owners were led to believe the dogs would be kept in the home, in a loving and safe environment.

One night, while the Hughes were in Florida, the air conditioning failed in the room where the dogs were kept. When Flake and his wife checked on the dogs at approximately 5:30 a.m., they discovered the air conditioner had gone out and many of the dogs had already died or were in serious distress, suffering from severe heat exhaustion. The couple did not make any emergency calls to a vet or seek aid from a veterinarian. According to the owners' own words, they never called a veterinarian and waited four hours to notify any of the pet owners, claiming that span of time was used for ongoing efforts to cool and resuscitate the dogs with water and ice.

Ultimately, twenty-three of the twenty-nine dogs died a horrible death.

During the investigation, the young Flakes made several contradictory claims to my lead investigator, Maria Trombi. She learned that the couple had lied to various dog owners, stating that their beloved family pets had gotten out and run away, avoiding having the conversation with them about what really happened. That fact was a significant factor in why my animal cruelty unit recommended charges against the Flake caretakers and the Hughes to the county attorney. Eventually, a grand jury agreed and charges were filed, including a felony count against all four.

The Flakes and Hughes told several owners their pets had escaped, and hid the fact that they died due to the failure of the air conditioner. They also claimed dogs opened a wall of the room by chewing through it and had severed an electrical cord supplying power to the air conditioning unit. Ultimately, the county attorney filed twenty-nine felony counts of animal cruelty against the Flakes and the Hughes. Additionally, the district attorney filed fraud charges for the misrepresentation of how the kennel was operated. The outrage in the community was intense, as it should have been.

Initially, several of my deputies didn't believe charges were warranted as the Flakes and the Hughes explained it away as if it was just a terrible tragedy. As Deputy Trombi continued to look into the case, the dog owners began a petition to charge the owners and operators of the kennel, and our department came under increasing pressure to conduct a criminal investigation.

Of significant importance to us was the deliberate and intentional misrepresentation of how the dogs were cared for and how they died. One owner, Shannon Gillette, had been promised by the Hughes of a kennel-free boarding house where no more than eight dogs were boarded at one time, even going so far as to boast on the kennel website of a "Disney World-like" experience for the dogs.

The morning of the incident, the Hughes left Gillette a voice mail message stating their two dogs had escaped via a hole dug under the fence by another dog. Gillette's mother stopped by the kennel as the rest of the family was scouring the neighborhood, only to find the dogs' bodies. One had blood coming from his eyes.

As the facts began to surface in the three-month investigation, and after a search warrant was served on the boarding facility, we had no choice but to recommend charges for all involved with 29 counts of animal cruelty that resulted in the deaths of 23 family pets. In an impromptu interview with MaLeisa Hughes in her front yard with a local Fox affiliate and several other media representatives, she was combative and made statements that conflicted with details given to my investigators. This interview enraged animal cruelty advocates and the grieving pet owners even more.

During grand jury testimony, the issue over the lack of maintenance of the air conditioning unit became a key piece of evidence. Since the Flakes had no control over the owners' air conditioner maintenance, charges against the Flakes were dropped, but the Hughes accepted a plea deal for 23 days in jail each (one day for each dog that died), along with 230 hours of community service. They agreed to never operate or work in an animal boarding facility in the future.

The Flakes' attorney claimed the lead investigator withheld critical evidence on the air conditioning maintenance and convinced the county attorney to drop charges against the Flakes. The defense argued the Flakes were operating on instructions from the Hughes on how to treat the dogs when discovered, including not calling a veterinarian. He also successfully argued no criminal charges could be filed as, under Arizona laws, the dogs could not be considered "victims" because they weren't human.

During the sentencing hearing a full two years later, wherein the dog owners were able to testify, Maricopa County Superior Judge Margaret Mahoney sentenced the Hughes to considerably longer sentences of 60 days each in jail, plus 230 hours of community service and three years' probation. They were ordered not to acquire any new animals, were banned from the kennel business, and ordered not to post any comments on the case on social media. The owners, however, created a Facebook page, which is still active today, calling the Hughes the Green Acres 23.

During this entire ordeal, Senator Flake was hounded by the media as the news made it into the national media, including protestors who showed up at a community speaking event to demand his son take responsibility. Flake had no choice but to make several public statements referring to the "accident" as a tragedy. Of course, my usual detractors claimed I used this opportunity to grab the spotlight by appearing at the scene of the crime, and made accusations that I was using the fact that Austin Flake was the son of a political enemy to pursue the case. But they could not explain how Senator Flake was an opponent, since we had never run against each other in a political race. Many accused the senator of exerting influence to get the judge to drop charges against his son, but no evidence was ever provided to that effect.

Former Arizona Senator Jeff Flake and I were never friends. Aside from the fact that Flake used every opportunity to criticize President Trump, a member of his own party, we never endorsed each other in any race either of us was in. Flake did donate $100 to my Democrat opponent and made sure to publicize the donation. And he and his family sued me in federal court, but it took only an hour for the court to rule in my favor.

Along with his buddy Mitt Romney (who asked for my endorsement during his presidential campaign), they have both turned out to be fake conservatives. The fact that Flake's family came under investigation for animal cruelty had nothing whatsoever to do with politics or the fact that we weren't each other's biggest fans.

Later, Flake's son Austin Flake and his wife sued me, investigator Trombi, and the Maricopa County Sheriff's Office for wrongful prosecution. Their attorneys also claimed investigator Trombi withheld key evidence on the air conditioner maintenance to the grand jury. While the department had a duty to investigate that charge, Trombi—an outstanding law enforcement investigator—was assigned desk duty and later on paid administrative leave, but she was ultimately cleared of any wrongdoing by the sheriff's office Professional Standards Bureau, which is akin to an internal affairs investigation.

During my six-hour deposition in the Flake son's civil wrongful prosecution suit, I was repeatedly asked about our investigation into Obama's birth certificate and our enforcement of immigration laws—both of which had nothing to do with Flake's claims. The plaintiff's attorney then placed the depositions on YouTube for all the world to see during my 2016 re-election campaign. It didn't bother me one bit, as I had nothing to hide, but it just goes to show how far my enemies will to go to try to demonize me and the sheriff's office.

The judge dismissed the case, then Flake's attorney appealed it to the Arizona Supreme Court, which rejected the case. The claims against investigator Trombi were also rejected and ultimately dismissed by both courts. Senator Flake made a big deal in the media that he donated the whopping amount of $100 to my Democratic opponent in 2016.

It's notable that the Flakes were willingly granted a jury trial—something I was never afforded in the Melendres case.

Sheriff Joe with rescued dogs

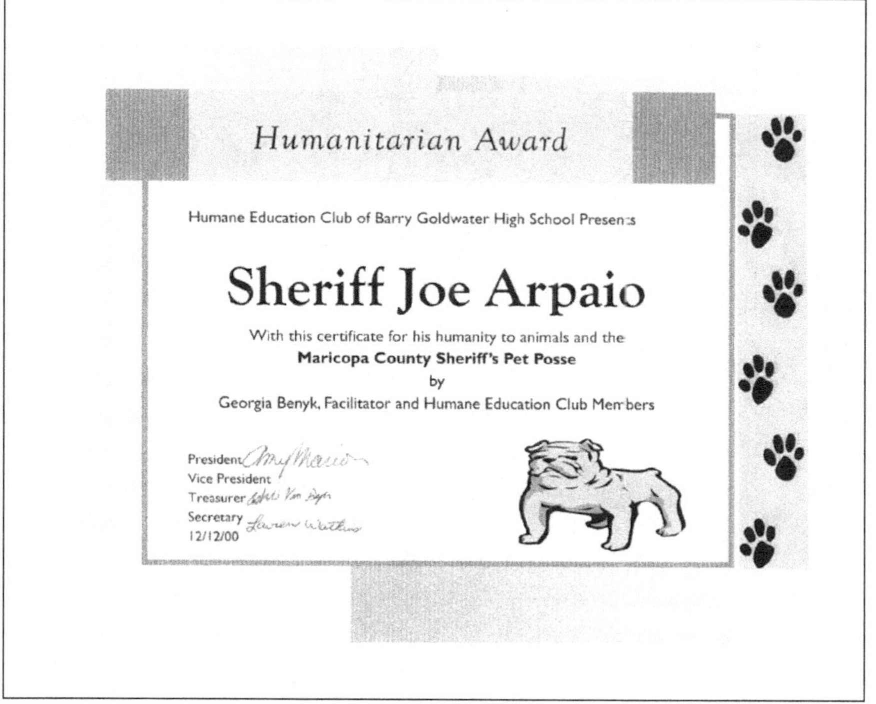

Humanitarian Award

Humane Education Club of Barry Goldwater High School Presents

Sheriff Joe Arpaio

With this certificate for his humanity to animals and the
Maricopa County Sheriff's Pet Posse
by
Georgia Benyk, Facilitator and Humane Education Club Members

President
Vice President
Treasurer
Secretary
12/12/00

Pet Posse Award—Sheriff Joe receives Humanitarian Award

HORSES HELP!

Special Community Award

Presented to

SHERIFF JOE ARPAIO

In Recognition and Appreciation
for Generosity and Commitment
to HORSES HELP

DATE 1-14-02 SIGNED Cindy Ramsey

SIGNED [illegible]

Special Community Award—Sheriff Joe receives Special Community Award

ELLIOT KATZ, DVM, PRESIDENT OF IN DEFENSE OF ANIMALS, AND THE ENTIRE MEMBERSHIP
OF
IN DEFENSE OF ANIMALS

PROUDLY ANNOUNCES

Sheriff Joe Arpaio

TO BE NAMED THE 2005 IN DEFENSE OF ANIMALS LIFETIME ACHIEVEMENT AWARD WINNER

For Sheriff Arpaios lifetime of courage and leadership in pursuing justice for animal victims of cruelty and neglect, for his vision in creating model programs to rehabilitate and find loving homes for animal victims in cruelty cases, and for Sheriff Arpaio's constant commitment to supporting the welfare of animals.

April 17, 2004

Elliot Katz, DVM,
President
In Defense of Animals

Defense of Animals—Sheriff Joe receives
Defense of Animals Lifetime Achievement Award

Presented to

SHERIFF JOE ARPAIO

April 9, 2005

The ***Compassion with Fashion*** Event
thanks you for your
dedication to the protection and care
of the precious animals of our communities

Arizona Humane Society—Sheriff Joe receives
Compassion with Fashion Certificate

Sheriff Joe and his dedication to rescued animals

CHAPTER 10

THE MELENDRES TRIAL CIRCUS

As America endured President Obama's first term in office, I became an obvious target for the open borders crowd. Because of the national attention I was getting in arresting illegal aliens and the growth of the largest sheriff's posse in the world, I became the top target for Attorney General Eric Holder and the Justice Department.

The fact that my programs were very popular in conservative and Republican circles certainly fanned those flames. While the Left was determined to grow their voting base by flooding the country with potential Democratic voters, I was simply trying to do my job by enforcing the laws already on the books. To me, this wasn't a political issue, but for them it became hyper-political.

Add in the fact that we began the investigation into the Obama birth certificate toward late 2011, making me public enemy number one to the Democrats, the ACLU, LA Raza, the Covington & Burling law firm, and George Soros. All of this would come into play during the ensuing and complex political witch hunt designed to remove me from office, inject fear into the Republicans, and to set a course that proved to be the playbook for the exact same type of coup attempt, with many of the same actors, used on President Trump.

In 2006, the Department of Homeland Security expanded Section 287(g) of the U.S. Immigration and Nationality Act to deputize state and local law enforcement officers to enforce federal immigration laws. This law was advanced by Attorney General John Ashcroft in 2002 after it was discovered that the 9-11 hijacking terrorists had entered the country on temporary visas and overstayed their expirations. The Bush administration felt that encouraging immigration enforcement cooperation with local law enforcement would add another layer to national security to thwart those who entered the country illegally or had overstayed their temporary visas. Personnel at these state and local offices were trained by U.S. Immigration and Customs Enforcement (ICE) originally to identify, process, and detain offenders of U.S. immigration law in the regular course of their law enforcement duties.

Even though the majority of local law enforcement officers did not participate in the training, more than 400,000 illegal aliens were deported as a result of 287(g). At a minimum, local law enforcement was encouraged to support 287(g) with respect to those being held in jail in order to check their immigration status. Resistance by some Democratic mayors, city councils, and county officials caused their locales to become known as "sanctuary cities." These local government bodies refused to check immigration status on those arrested, commonly letting criminal illegal aliens back on the streets to commit heinous crimes such as pedophilia, rape, and even murder.

It was no secret that President Obama intended to pursue more of an open-border policy after this election, spearheaded by his Attorney General Eric Holder. It was very clear to us and law enforcement all over the country that the events of 9-11 taught us that law enforcement at all levels needed to cooperate with federal immigration officials in the battle against terrorism. How could we keep our country safe if we didn't know who was coming in and who had overstayed their welcome?

Under 287(g), I signed a contract with the head of ICE at my office to assist with the enforcement of immigration laws in Maricopa County. Upon execution of that agreement, 160 officers that were qualified were then trained for six months by DHS, technically as ICE agents. Originally, DHS wanted to put ICE agents in our office; however, I would not approve that request, instead believing training and deputizing my officers was a better solution than installing federal agents within the sheriff's office.

Our Memorandum of Understanding (MOA) agreement, executed in January of 2007, specifically stated:

> *It is the intent of the parties that these delegated authorities will enable the LEA (law enforcement agency or, in this case, the Maricopa County Sheriff's Office) to "identify" and process immigration violators in Maricopa County consistent with the terms of this MOA.*

Further, it goes on to state the assignments:

> *Before participating, LEA personnel receive authorization to perform immigration officer functions granted under this MOA, they must successfully complete mandatory 5-week (4-week for LEA personnel functioning solely in a correctional*

facility or ICE detention facility) training in the enforcement of federal immigration laws and policies as provided by ICE instructors and thereafter pass examinations equivalent to those given to ICE officers. Only participating LEA personnel who are selected, trained, authorized, and supervised, as set out herein, have authority pursuant to this MOA to conduct the immigration officer functions enumerated in this MOA.

Participating LEA personnel performing immigration-related duties pursuant to this MOA will be LEA officers assigned to the Violent Fugitive Apprehension Squad, Criminal Investigations Section, Anti-Gang Unit, Drug Enforcement Unit, and Community Action Teams. Participating LEA personnel will be exercising their immigration-related authorities during the course of criminal investigations involving aliens encountered within Maricopa County. Any combination of these officers or others may be assigned and/or co-located as task force officers to assist ICE agents with criminal investigations.

These authorized functions granted in the MOA included:

The power and authority to interrogate any alien or person believed to be an alien as to his right to be or remain in the United States and to process for immigration violations those individuals who are convicted of State or Federal felony offenses.

The power to arrest without warrant any alien entering or attempting to unlawfully enter the United States, or any alien in the United States, if the officer has reason to believe the alien to be arrested is in the United States in violation of the law and is likely to escape before a warrant can be obtained.

The power to serve warrants of arrest for immigration violations.

The power and authority to detain and transport arrested aliens to ICE-approved detention facilities.

The MOA also dictated the level of ICE supervision:

Immigration enforcement activities conducted by the participating LEA personnel will be supervised and directed by ICE supervisory officers or the designated team leader in Phoenix. Participating LEA personnel are not authorized to perform immigration officer functions, except when working under the supervision of an ICE officer.

During this period, when we were operating under the supervision of ICE, not one time did the Maricopa County Sheriff's Office or any of our deputies come under review, either by my office or by ICE, for violating the MOA. The MOA and our training were very clear that race could be used as "one" criterion used by officers in the field when combined with "probable" cause. My deputies were never taught, encouraged, or advised to pull someone over on a traffic stop just for being Hispanic or for the appearance of being from Mexican descent.

When Arizona passed State Law SB 1070, it had reverberations throughout the country. Arizona was besieged with crime emanating from criminal gangs coming in from Mexico and Central America. Phoenix became the American capital for kidnapping for ransom and for human smuggling. State officials and law enforcement (including me) begged the federal government to seal the border. The Obama administration was highly critical of the legislation. With former Governor Janet Napolitano then at the head of the Department of Homeland Security, they were determined to reign in our efforts to reduce crime caused by illegal immigration. While governor of Arizona, Napolitano fought every piece of state legislation to curb illegal immigration before she left to join the Obama administration.

By 2010, the Obama administration was livid over Tent City Jails, pink underwear, the chain gangs, and our successful use of the posse in the successful interdiction of illegal immigration under the 287(g) program. The fact was that our programs were popular with the majority of Arizonans, and were a beacon of light for other border states in how to attack the problem.

Between the Obama administration, the ACLU, La Raza, and dozens of other radical organizations, they all were primed to look for any and all opportunities to curb our success. The federal government sued Arizona over SB 1070 and were effective in watering down the original legislation somewhat, but it didn't impact our ability to enforce immigration law under SB 1070 or under 287(g). Our opponents began to openly "shop around" for enough complaints to file a lawsuit, going back to a 2007 incident that started this entire decade of court cases, wasting millions of dollars on both sides. Spurred by an Obama Justice Department lawsuit against the Maricopa County Sheriff's Office, they found their avenue.

The Obama administration kept up its efforts to curb our enforcement of these laws via investigations through the Department of Justice. But, even in 2012, the U.S. attorney from the District of Arizona closed her investigation of our practices due to no findings of criminal conduct.

My deputies showed up at a day laborer location after complaints from citizens in the community. Several of these individuals were, in fact, illegal but one (Mr. Melendres), who could not produce documentation, was also taken into custody until his legal status could be ascertained. It is important to remember that many times my deputies were given fake government documents by these individuals that were so poorly created that our trained deputies could make that determination right away.

Mr. Melendres, allegedly a U.S. citizen, spent several hours at the Maricopa County Jail before being released and, after seeking counsel, his attorneys, who also contacted the ACLU and the Mexican-American Legal Defense and Education Fund (MALDEF), decided to file a class action lawsuit against the sheriff's office. Joining them was the law firm Covington & Burling, a Washington, D.C. law firm. This is the same law firm that fought for the Deferred Action for Childhood Arrivals (DACA) in the Ninth Circuit and in which Eric Holder was an attorney and today is a partner. This is also the same firm of Lanny Breuer, the head of Holder's Justice Department Criminal Division, and one active in many Democratic causes. Breuer was also at the center of the "Fast and Furious" scandal within the Department of Justice that resulted in an illegal gun operation and the death of a U.S. Border Patrol agent. When Breuer left the Department of Justice, he returned to private practice at Covington & Burling.

The attorneys sought a class action lawsuit in which the media portrayed thousands of alleged racially profiled victims of the Maricopa County Sheriff's Office. The fact of the matter is that the Melendres class action lawsuit had but five original individual plaintiffs, in which two were eventually dropped when it was proven that no racial profiling occurred in their arrests. The other lone plaintiff was a community organizer group named Somos America. In the hundreds of thousands of arrests that the Maricopa County Sheriff's Office conducted during this period, there were only three individual plaintiffs who came forward to allege some kind of injustice.

But make no mistake; the media, the ACLU, Mexican-American Legal Defense and Education Fund (MALDEF), and the Obama Justice Department were fanning the flames to mis-characterize the significant role the Maricopa County Sheriff's Office was playing in assisting ICE with the deportation of thousands of illegals and stemming the tide of human smuggling in Arizona. The sensationalism became so ridiculous that many of our crime sweeps that ultimately led to the arrest of countless illegal aliens were deemed to be "Hispanic hunting" by these same groups. The media coverage was as blinding as it was unfair to the Maricopa County Sheriff's Office—and to me.

It was alleged that efforts were organized under cooperation from multiple sources against the deportation of illegal aliens to place U.S. citizens with Mexican-American or Hispanic heritage in vehicles and bust out the tail lights so they would get stopped upon receiving leaked tips that we were about to perform "saturation raids" in areas where we knew illegals were going to day laborer sites. The obvious intent was to have U.S. citizens detained, then make public and take whatever actions they could to end our practices. We were never able to determine in court testimony whether Melendres was one of these "setups."

Of course, one cannot underestimate the fact that Arizona has remained a "battleground state" when it comes to national or presidential politics. The millions and millions of dollars that have flowed into Arizona from Soros and others on the Left have (and still have) a dual purpose—to destroy enforcement of illegal immigration laws in an effort to provide amnesty for illegals and encourage open borders, and to mobilize political forces to turn Arizona permanently "blue."

The Obama administration began investigations into the Maricopa County Sheriff's Office almost as soon as he was sworn in. I'm sure I was high on his and Attorney General Eric Holder's contempt list and, ultimately, I refused to cooperate. After three years, despite their access to thousands of documents and Maricopa County Sheriff's Office employees, they complained of being stonewalled. The truth is they kept asking the same questions and kept getting the same answers. Under Holder's orders, the Department of Homeland Security removed the Maricopa County Sheriff's Office—the most successful local law enforcement agency in the 287(g) program in the country—from the 287(g) program.

That was the only dog-whistle the radicals needed. In September 2012, under the direction of the ACLU, a class action lawsuit was filed in federal court claiming the Maricopa County Sheriff's Office racially profiled Hispanics. Originally, this case was assigned to U.S. District Judge Mary Murguia, a Clinton appointee, who then, at the request of my attorneys, recused herself due to her sister holding a leadership position with La Raza. This case was then assigned to Federal Judge G. Murray Snow, a George W. Bush appointee. We always wondered if we wouldn't have been better off with Judge Murguia.

Ultimately, Judge Snow ruled against us. We immediately

appealed to the ultra-liberal 9th Circuit Court of Appeals and, as expected, they also ruled against us. Judge Snow issued a rambling 59-page ambiguous order for change in our policies that was impossible on its face to implement or follow. In fact, the current sheriff is still not compliant, principally because the order is written so poorly and because rank-and-file officers remain confused about the protocols in the order.

In subsequent interviews I conducted with the media, I was asked if the Maricopa County Sheriff's Office would continue to enforce immigration laws. Of course, I answered in the affirmative, because there were still state immigration laws that I was required to enforce. The Obama administration had pulled our MOA regarding 287(g); however, in order to avoid becoming a sanctuary city, we still cooperated with ICE and kept detainers on arrested individuals who were proven to be illegal for ICE to pick up and later deport. We issued thousands of detainers during my tenure as sheriff, issuing more than 10,000 in my last two years in office alone.

During this period, the Obama administration was using "consent decrees" to effectively "federalize" local enforcement to their will under Assistant Attorney General Tom Perez (now the head of the Democratic National Committee) via the threat of a civil or criminal complaint that could cost taxpayers millions of dollars. The effort was centered around intervening in local practices when it came to immigration enforcement. Perez would come to Arizona just to conduct press conferences, timed before court appearances, to allege my office was conducting racial profiling. Perez later claimed that I was "President Trump's version of law or order," attempting to somehow link our efforts in enforcing laws with their claim that President Trump was racist.

The Maricopa County Sheriff's Office became the "poster child" for this effort, resulting in the civil contempt and eventual criminal contempt case. This was the proverbial "shot across the bow" at the most publicly-known sheriff's office (and the highest-profile immigration enforcement sheriff) that would be used to intimidate other local law enforcement organizations during the Obama administration and beyond.

My opponents never want to talk about the fact that about one-third of these deportees would end up back in my jails. It was a revolving door, due to the lack of desire by the Obama administration to enforce immigration laws. Traffic stops also have a huge impact on solving crimes. How many criminals, who have had bodies in the trunks of their cars, or been loaded with huge stashes of illegal drugs, were terrorists, or were pedophiles transporting juveniles? For the same reason we find and arrest those criminals during routine traffic stops, it is essential for one of my deputies to discover if someone is in the country illegally when they get pulled over for a burned-out taillight or a missing license plate.

This is one of the reasons that I was never a fan of red light cameras. Red light cameras can't do routine police work and are only used as a revenue-generating gimmick. A red-light camera would never discover a terrorist, kidnapper, rapist, or murderer, but good cops on routine traffic stops will usually have their instincts triggered and many times make arrests when a crime may have not been solved by any other means. The bogus charges that our deputies would pull over someone just for being Hispanic or a minority were laughable and, in fact, unequivocally not proven during the trial.

Throughout my career, I always took responsibility for my deputies and officers, which is why I prefer taking the tough questions myself in our public press conferences. I believe in full transparency and I prefer that my constituents hear the facts from me.

Later, we would find out that Judge Snow was incensed over the interviews I conducted after the trial and perceived them as an attack on him. He also was irritated over recordings of training sessions where a deputy might have said something derogatory about the judge or the ambiguous order, which they have a First Amendment right to do.

But the case in Snow's court took dramatic swings. It came to my attention by multiple credible sources that Judge Snow's wife was overheard at a restaurant saying that her husband would use the ACLU case before him to destroy me. Judge Snow has never refuted that claim by his wife. The judge hated me and would to anything to get me out of office. He even called me to the witness stand during trial and began to interrogate me about this matter, as if he was the prosecutor. This was highly irregular. Because of his wife's claim he should have recused himself from the case.

Moreover, the media played up the fact that I've gone after other county and state officials for corruption, both Democrats and Republicans. I'm sworn to uphold the law. It doesn't matter to me who it is, even if there is a question on the legitimacy of a government document that warrants an investigation on the president of the United States!

Secondly, as previously mentioned, the Obama birth certificate investigation was ongoing, even during the Snow trial. Our paid informant in that investigation, alleged NSA whistleblower Dennis Montgomery, was introduced to us by Blixseth, as previously mentioned. Montgomery, through Blixseth, had come to us with credible information about the identity theft of more than 150,000 Maricopa County residents.

We were shown actual evidence that Maricopa County residents' personal identity information was contained in the data Montgomery allegedly liberated from government computers while he was working as a subcontractor for the NSA. My investigation never determined how Montgomery acquired that information. Montgomery maintained it was collected by federal government agencies such as the CIA, NSA and the FBI, all running clandestine spying operations that surreptitiously breached various computer networks such as phone and internet companies, major banks, Wall Street investment firms, and the IRS to gather American citizens' most personal information.

JOE ARPAIO BRIEF
Timeline

Date	Description	Breach IP Address	Time Call	From Call	To Call	Duration in (Min)
2001 - 2008	Eric Holder Senior Partner Covington Burling Law Firm					
2001 – 2009	Lanny Breuer Senior Partner Covington Burling Law Firm					
02/12/07	ACLU Files Melendres Lawsuit Against Arpaio					
06/15/08	US Department of Justice (DOJ) announces investigation into Joe Arpaio					
02/01/09	US Department of Justice (DOJ) - Hires Eric Holder Attorney General US					
03/15/09	Arizona Attorney General (AG) Issues Search Warrant Deputy Joel Fox					
04/20/09	Lanny Breuer Hired As Assistant AG Criminal Div. - DOJ					
07/07/09	Joe Arpaio Announces he will not cooperate with DOJ Investigation					
07/15/09	US Federal Judge Mary Murguia recuses herself from the Arpaio case.					
07/20/09	US Department of Justice (DOJ) - Calls Federal Judge G. Murray Snow			202.514.2000	602.322.7560	10
07/22/09	Judge G. Murray Snow Assigned To Arpaio Federal Cases (Not Random)					
07/23/09	US Department of Justice (DOJ) - Calls Federal Judge G. Murray Snow			202.514.2000	602.322.7560	32
09/01/09	John Gray Starts Intern Clerk Job with Federal Judge G. Murray Snow					
09/16/09	Dennis Burke Becomes US Attorney General Arizona					
09/25/09	US Department of Justice (DOJ) - Calls Dennis Burke US Attorney Arizona		10:43	202.514.2000	602.514.7500	9
09/26/09	Judge G. Murray Snow Calls US Department of Justice (DOJ)		11:04	602.322.7560	202.514.2000	16
09/28/09	Dennis Burke US Attorney - Calls Judge G. Murray Snow		11:44	602.514.7500	602.322.7560	6
09/28/09	US Department of Justice (DOJ) - Wire Tap #56990-34 Block 602-920-4000,++					
10/15/09	US Gov breached Maricopa all domains, and subdomains	156.42.184.18				
	Maricopa Government - mcao.maricpoa.gov - mcso.maricopa.gov	156.42.184.65				
	Mail servers: extmail1.maricopa.gov extmail2.maricopa.gov	156.42.103.166				
03/25/10	Federal Judge Mary Murguia nominated to the 9th Circuit Court Appeals.					
05/24/10	US Department of Justice (DOJ) - Civil Rights Calls Federal Judge G. Murray Snow			202.514.6225	602.322.7560	14
05/28/10	DOJ Criminal Division Wire Tap #64402-03 602-920-4400, 602-920-4000					
08/15/10	US Gov breached Maricopa all domains, and subdomains	156.42.184.18				
	Maricopa Government - mcao.maricpoa.gov - mcso.maricopa.gov	156.42.184.65				
	Mail servers: extmail1.maricopa.gov extmail2.maricopa.gov	156.42.103.166				
07/10/10	Covington Burling Law Firm Take Over Melendres Lawsuit Against Arpaio.					
09/02/10	US Department of Justice (DOJ) files suit against Arpaio					
09/15/10	US Department of Justice (DOJ) Call Federal Judge G. Murray Snow			202.307.0652	602.322.7560	5

Confidential Information Not to Be Disclosed — Rev 1.5a

JOE ARPAIO BRIEF
Timeline

Date	Description	Breach IP Address	Time Call	From Call	To Call	Duration in (Min)
09/15/10	John Gray Ends Intern Clerk with Federal Judge G. Murray Snow					
10/01/10	John Gray Joins Perkins Coie Law Firm					
10/18/10	Covington Burling Law Firm Call Department of Justice (DOJ) - Not In This Case		14:55	650.632.4704	202.514.6225	10
10/22/10	Covington Burling Law Firm Call Perkins Coie (John Gray)		14:21	650.632.4704	602.351.8092	19
10/23/10	US Government Breached - www.jshfirm.com mail.jshfirm.com	216.119.127.142				
	Service25-us.mimecast.com ; service26-us.mimecast.com					
10/25/10	US Department of Justice (DOJ) Calls Perkins Coie (John Gray)		16:30	202.514.2000	602.351.8092	8
10/25/10	Perkins Coie Associate (John Gray) makes call to Federal Judge Snow Chambers		16:42	602.351.8092	602.322.7560	10
10/25/10	Perkins Coie Associate (John Gray) makes call to Maricopa County Cell Phone ++		16:55	602.351.8092	602.+++	4
01/04/11	US Federal Judge Mary Murguia approved as 9th Circuit Court of Appeals Judge					
04/23/11	Sheriff Arpaio Fires Chief Deputy David Hendershott and Deputy Larry Black					
08/30/11	Dennis Burke Resigns As Us Attorney Arizona - Fast and Furious Scandal					
10/21/11	Sheriff Arpaio Fires MSCO Captain Joel Fox					
09/01/11	US Department of Justice (DOJ) files complaint against Sheriff Arpaio					
07/19/12	Melendres vs. Sheriff Arpaio Trial Heard by Federal Judge G. Murray Snow					
03/01/13	Lanny Breuer Resigns from DOJ and rejoins Covington Burling Law Firm					
06/13/13	US Department of Justice (DOJ) Joins Melendres Lawsuit with Covington Law Firm					
10/02/13	Judge G. Murray Snow Rules in Class Action Lawsuit Against Joe Arpaio					

Red - Phone Calls made to or from the Department of Justice
Green - John Gray Interns for Federal Judge G. Murray Snow (2009 - 2010)
Blue - Judge G. Murray Snow Assigned To Arpaio Federal Case

Confidential Information Not to Be Disclosed — Rev 1.5a

The initial information provided to us proved to be authentic and had the potential to be used in all types of identity theft crimes that could result in thousands of my residents being victimized if I didn't stop this information from falling into the wrong hands. When we tried to introduce this evidence in federal court, Judge Snow, whose personal information was in the database that Montgomery turned over, wrongly interpreted this as though we were investigating *him*.

When investigator Zullo reviewed this information for the first time in late 2013, he was able to identify my name and information and his name and information, along with a host of others in the sheriff's office, even members of Congress, in Montgomery's files. The information was allegedly collected between 2000-2010. The data presented to us as evidence was real. Montgomery's claim regarding its acquisition had yet to be deemed credible. Based on this information, I opened an identity theft investigation to protect citizens and get to the bottom of the source of the Montgomery information.

We then went to Arizona State Attorney General Tom Horne with Montgomery to explain the data he had on these 150,000 residents. Horne agreed to provide Montgomery with immunity from prosecution, provided that he testified under oath. Montgomery was subsequently interviewed for six hours at the attorney general's office by Detective Mackiewicz, Zullo and Arizona State attorney general officials. Montgomery laid out in detail the government's illegal spying operation and violation of American citizens' constitutional rights. It is important to keep in mind that, as you are reading this book, you may be aware of some of this today because of current media reports, but back in

2013 no one had any vast public knowledge or awareness of this type of intrusive activity and the term "Deep State" had not yet become the buzzword it is today.

Based on Montgomery's representations I now had a bigger problem on my hands—illegal activity by the federal government agencies and violations of millions of American citizens constitutional rights not only in Arizona, but the entire nation. I was ultimately concerned with national security and now that this information had landed in my lap it was important to me to get it—or Montgomery—to the right people to expose it and to mitigate any unconstitutional acts that were being committed against American citizens. Certainly, we believed that the FBI would be interested in this information.

Normally this would have been brought to the FBI; however, Montgomery refused to work with the FBI. I did not have enough credible information to bring it forward without Montgomery as a material witness. And, according to Montgomery, the FBI was part of the problem. And I still had 150,000 residents to protect.

I decided to proceed forward and assigned Mackiewicz and Zullo to the Montgomery case. Our strategy early on was to relieve Montgomery of as much information as possible and eventually turn it over to federal authorities. Montgomery agreed to download the purported sensitive government information onto approximately 50 hard drives over the next six months. Montgomery produced drives that he claimed included not only privileged government documents but also the computer source code that would prove the information was obtained via a government clandestine computer system known as the "Hammer." He also emphasized that the information on the drives was so sensitive in nature it could not be viewed by anyone that did not have the proper government security clearance. As Montgomery produced the hard drives over time, each drive was taken as it was produced and sealed in an evidence box and placed under high security at my office for months.

Little did I know that later on in the investigation Montgomery would not only produce all this sensitive information but he would bring forward a bombshell. He alleged he had records that showed communication between Judge Snow and Eric Holder's office before and *during* my trial! I did nothing with this information but a leak from my office to a local newspaper would set off a firestorm.

Throughout this entire ordeal with Montgomery, he continued to provide us "kernels" of truth, with just enough information to keep the investigation alive and his paid informant status current until the next check was due. Despite the fact that Zullo and my staff were extremely skeptical of Montgomery, he provided us just enough information to continue to lead us on. In the meantime, the intelligence community both praised Montgomery and ridiculed him as a con man. One thing was for sure, Montgomery continued to implicate John Brennan and James Clapper in every conspiracy plot he presented to us.

As time went on, Zullo and Mackiewicz briefed me on the progress of Montgomery. Zullo told me that Montgomery had a hot button issue. He wanted to get immunity as a whistleblower with a federal judge. My investigators were concerned that, if Montgomery did in fact have Top Secret Information, we had a duty to bring it to federal authorities.

We were also advised at that time that, under federal criminal statutes, now that we knew the possibility of this evidence existed, we had to present it either to the FBI or a federal judge.

Zullo and I believed I that we absolutely had to get Montgomery and his information to federal authorities to prove whether it was all he said it was—or not. Zullo believed he could make this happen and presented his idea to me. He wanted to enlist the help of attorney Larry Klayman. Larry had been a friend to Zullo and me stemming back to the beginning of the birth certificate investigation. Klayman had just won a legal victory over the NSA that shut down the agency's bulk telephony metadata collection program. Zullo knew Klayman would be very interested in Montgomery. He also knew that Klayman had a connection to a sitting federal judge in D.C.

Zullo's plan was that we ask Klayman to represent Montgomery for the purpose of bringing Montgomery and his information before a federal judge. Zullo argued that this would force Montgomery to produce any credible information that we were not permitted to see due to security clearance issues and have it verified if it actually existed. And, once he did, it would just be a matter of time before Montgomery would be forced into a position to work with the FBI and we would be done with him. I agreed and authorized Zullo to make contact with Klayman.

After a series of meetings, Larry Klayman arranged a meeting with respected Federal Judge Royce D. Lamberth, who sat as the presiding judge on the secretive FISA court from 1995-2002. Supposedly, Judge Lamberth was a key figure in the FISA court who authorized wiretaps that eventually led to Osama Bin Laden.

I dispatched Mackiewicz and Zullo on three occasions to travel to D.C. along with Klayman for meetings with Judge

Lamberth in D.C., including one meeting where we brought Montgomery before the judge. Montgomery came into the meeting with a file full of documents that neither of my investigators had seen. Montgomery handed Judge Lamberth page after page from the file with certain data on it, not showing to the others in the meeting.

It was obvious by the judge's reaction after reviewing one document in particular that there was something to all of this. One of the documents handed over to the judge by Montgomery was described as illegal wiretap information. The document had about 40 phone numbers and corresponding serial numbers on it, and one of them was mine!

Montgomery also claimed it had other Maricopa County Sheriff's Office officials' phones that had been illegally surveilled as well. Zullo, reported back to me that, during the meeting, Judge Lamberth looked at that document, placed it face up on the conference table, placed his right hand on top of it and looked Zullo directly in the eye and, with a stone-cold poker face, said "There is not a FISA court in the nation that would have authorized this. Joe Arpaio is no terrorist!"

Zullo said it appeared that the judge recognized what was on the document, which was surveillance of me. Obviously, the judge did find something credible in the information because he asked for a little time to decide on just how and to whom to bring this to in the federal government.

It was times like this that would keep us working with Montgomery. Every so often he would produce something that had some merit to it. But, for the most part, it was few and far between.

Mackiewicz and Zullo had a third follow-up meeting with the judge and Klayman in D.C. My investigators wanted to be certain that it was the judge's understanding that we could not vouch for the credibility of the information, or Montgomery himself, because they had not seen privileged information nor had we investigated it. They told the judge they would continue to make every attempt to validate Montgomery's claims until such time as they could no longer do so or federal authorities took over.

Zullo had expressed to me his increasing skepticism and outright distrust of Montgomery going back some months. He spent hours upon hours in conversation with Montgomery. He and Detective Mackiewicz would catch Montgomery lying to them multiple times. Frustrated by Montgomery's never-ending, overpromising, and constant failure to deliver as promised, coupled with the caveat of secrecy placed on the content of 50 hard drives of data, Zullo decided to start at the beginning looking for inconsistencies in Montgomery's story.

One evening Zullo re-watched the taped interview of Montgomery taken at the Arizona attorney general's office almost a year earlier. It was in that interview that Montgomery made a comment that would prove to be his undoing with my office.

During the interview, Montgomery represented himself as the sole person responsible for the creation of not only the illegal hacking software and the computer system known as the "Hammer," that could surreptitiously breach any computer around the globe and download or upload any information at will, he also claimed to be the person that developed the "harvesting" software responsible for mass data collection of information on every American citizen by the U.S. government. Being that this was alleged to be a secret government program, it was all but impossible to confirm or disprove. It would, however, prove later on to be false.

During the interview, Montgomery made one fleeting statement that grabbed Zullo's attention. Montgomery stated that there were other whistleblowers who came forward in early 2000, but that nothing came of it. That cursory statement prompted Zullo to further investigate and ultimately discover the identities of the three individuals, all former NSA employees turned whistleblowers, who actually created the harvesting software for the NSA that Montgomery was falsely taking credit for. It was not Dennis Montgomery. This revelation was alarming. Montgomery's story was about to fall apart.

Bill Binney, Kirk Wiebe, and Thomas Drake were all former NSA employees who worked to develop the NSA mass harvesting computer software system known as "Thin Thread." This software could sort through and collect massive amounts of data originally designed to identify and target threat-related communications jeopardizing national security. It could separate these communications and encrypt them to protect the Fourth Amendment constitutional protections of all U.S. citizens. Only with a warrant from a FISA court could this information be unencrypted and viewed by government authorities.

This program was later stripped of its Fourth Amendment encryption protections and morphed into a program, called "Trailblazer," which would collect vast amounts of data completely unencrypted. This constitutional abuse prompted these former NSA employees to turn whistleblowers.

Zullo arranged a meeting at my office where he laid out his

findings and concerns, and made a bold request. He wanted my permission to locate the former NSA employees, enlist their assistance, and have them inspect the hard drives that Montgomery claimed contained Top Secret information. Zullo no longer believed there was anything of value on the drives Montgomery had created months earlier. And this would be the only way to verify the content and confirm Montgomery's credibility.

After much deliberation I agreed and authorized Zullo and Mackiewicz to locate these men to set up a meeting to enlist their help. A meeting date was set and I dispatched Zullo and Mackiewicz to Maryland for the meeting.

Binny, Wiebe and Drake agreed to inspect the drives. Zullo and Mackiewicz left with the drives headed to Maryland with a standing order. If, at any time, anything remotely classified was located on the drives, they were to stop inspecting the drives, package them up and drive right to the FBI in Washington, D.C. and turn it over immediately.

Mackiewicz and Zullo traveled to Maryland, to the home of Kirk Wiebe, with the hard drive evidence to be reviewed. Wiebe, Binney and Drake began to inspect the drives in the presence of my investigators. Over the next five hours, drive after drive was opened. And, as Zullo suspected, there was nothing of value or top-secret information on any of it.

It was all garbage!

Wiebe and Drake issued a devastating report where they determined, in their expert opinion, that Montgomery was a fraud. None of the information could be sourced back to origin and what was placed on the drives was thousands of pages of pure nonsense. When advised of this disappointing development,

I terminated Montgomery's Confidential Informant agreement with my office.

Montgomery was over as far as I was concerned but there was still one nagging problem. Montgomery did have some verifiable information that he brought to my office in the beginning—the private identity information of 150,000 Maricopa County residents and millions of people across the nation. He had pages of banking records, account passwords, and a host of other data. He also had the private cell and other information of one Donald J. Trump, a billionaire who would later become the 45th president of the United States three short years later. I had to do something about this.

I shut down the Montgomery investigation, but authorized Zullo to monitor Montgomery's activities from a distance. We believed that Montgomery would ultimately be forced to work with the FBI and, if not, I would bring this to the FBI without Montgomery. Some six months later, this was precisely what happened.

After the judge learned what Montgomery allegedly had, which was supposedly a treasure trove of information about the illegal surveillance of American citizens, he connected Montgomery with FBI Director James Comey and FBI General Counsel James Baker to expose Obama and intelligence chiefs John Brennan and James Clapper. It's unlikely at the time that Judge Lamberth, who had previously served on the FISA court, had any indication of how corrupt the FBI had become under Comey.

Montgomery began cooperating with FBI Director James Comey, allegedly providing evidence to his general counsel that

American intelligence agencies have been illegally harvesting financial and other records of Supreme Court justices and other judges, prominent business titans, and others for blackmail purposes using "The Hammer, which reportedly was provided with full knowledge of its intended purposes by Robert Mueller.

In two subsequent conversations between Zullo and Montgomery, Montgomery advised Zullo that the FBI wanted some documentation that was verifiable before they would give Montgomery any type of immunity. Montgomery told Zullo he gave the FBI's James Baker the illegal wiretap information of my cell phones to verify. It was the same information that, only a few short months before, Judge Lamberth appeared to recognize in a face-to-face meeting with my investigators. Montgomery claimed that, based on that exact evidence, the FBI proceeded to grant him immunity.

Why that statement of immunity by the judge is critical was that, prior to evidence released by famed whistleblower Edward Snowden, James Clapper and others in the "Deep State" intelligence agencies had testified that they never spied on American citizens. The original intent of establishing the FISA courts after 9-11 was to spy on terrorists who may have had communications with fellow terrorists or American citizens and not communications and other data related to the average American and certainly not to weaponize for political reasons.

Judge Lamberth went on to say at the same meeting with investigator Zullo, attorney Larry Klayman, and Dennis Montgomery, along with Montgomery's son-in-law and Klayman's legal assistant, "And certainly Sheriff Joe is no terrorist," indicating his obvious disgust at the evidence he had in his hands.

Throughout this entire ordeal with Montgomery, he continued to provide us "kernels" of truth, with just enough information to keep the investigation alive and his paid informant status current until the next check was due. Despite the fact that Zullo and my staff were extremely skeptical of Montgomery, he would provide us just enough information to continue to lead us on. In the meantime, the intelligence community both praised Montgomery and ridiculed him as a con man. One thing was for sure, Montgomery continued to implicate John Brennan and James Clapper in every conspiracy plot he presented to us.

After this information was provided to Judge Lamberth, we had no further contact directly with Montgomery on the evidence, as Klayman was brokering the interactions between the FBI and Montgomery. Montgomery and other FBI officials would eventually face Congressional committee hearings, where many additional and disturbing details would emerge and which still dominate current news cycles.

During this entire period, neither myself nor investigator Zullo received any FBI or NSA inquiries into the nature of our investigation. Zero. None. You would think the FBI and the intelligence agencies would want to know what we knew or to follow-up on the leads that Montgomery supposedly provided.

In the meantime, we were beginning to be cast as hapless "keystone cops," out of our league for both this investigation and for the Obama birth certificate investigation. The goal of the opposition was to make us appear irrelevant and in over our heads. I may have been a county sheriff at the time, but they seriously underestimated my background in dealing with international crime and the inner workings of the intelligence apparatus

I worked with on a daily basis in Turkey, the Middle East and Mexico. There likely hasn't been a United States sheriff in history with the background and experience I have in law enforcement. I was not simply going to "go away."

Had the NSA lost control of this alleged rogue whistleblower?

As far as we know, Montgomery never got immunity for his wiretap information. Was there some other deal cut with Comey or others? Possibly, but maybe this will come out in the current investigations by the U.S. attorney general. If, in fact, President Trump ever pardons whistleblower Edward Snowden (which is not certain to happen), the dominos could certainly fall—and fall quickly—at the very highest levels of the intelligence community and could even include former White House officials.

As fate would have it, when I sued CNN TV host Chris Cuomo, the Huffington Post, and Rolling Stone over disparaging and factually incorrect statements made about me on air regarding my pardon, and calling me a "convicted felon," the case landed in Lamberth's court. Certainly, I felt Lamberth would give us a fair hearing, but he dismissed the case, citing "the defendant never articulated proof of malice," publicly stating a known misrepresentation of the fact that I was prosecuted for criminal contempt (a misdemeanor) and not a felony. That statement by Cuomo was no accident.

It appeared that, every time we were in court, no matter what judge, we were in the quintessential "star chamber" known in English law (and made famous under the reign of Henry VII), to be highly secretive, politically motivated, and rotten to the core.

Our original appeals into the Justice Department's lawsuit and the Melendres class action suit predictably fell on deaf ears in the ultra-liberal 9th Circuit Court of Appeals in San Francisco. Maricopa County originally set aside $350,000 for victim compensation based on the amount of time a class action claimant spent in actual custody. It was later increased to $500,000. It has been reported that the costs of complying with Judge Snow's and the Justice Department's orders have allegedly cost Maricopa taxpayers nearly $140 million, with many of these fees going to Judge Snow's brother-in-law's employer, Covington & Burling. As mentioned earlier, Snow would not recuse himself from this case despite the obvious conflict of interest. That fact alone should have been enough for the 9th Circuit to send to re-trial.

The total number of claimants on the class action lawsuit, which had a 2018 deadline to file a claim, was only three that we could find in any public documents. It's likely that less than $10,000.00 was paid out. Even after tons of advertising in Mexico and Central America by the ACLU and the other plaintiffs in the case, the end result was a complete dud. No claimants came forward to claim a piece of the class action lawsuit, simply because the charges were bogus to begin with. Of course, you never hear any more about this in the news because it was such a flop. But you do hear a lot of noise used against me because of the cost of compliance laid out by the Holder Justice Department. The fact that the current sheriff is still dealing with non-compliance and associated costs is a testament to how poorly Judge Snow's order was crafted.

My opponents always like to throw out these large numbers for county defense work from these and other cases. The truth of the matter is that, many times, the Maricopa County Board of Supervisors didn't have the backbone to stand up to frivolous lawsuits and too quickly tried to settle early or to countersue. When you have a history of appeasement in court cases, good plaintiff attorneys, like sharks, can smell blood in the water for miles.

Most of the money in this case, as in many other cases, went to the attorneys. The final number of alleged plaintiffs awarded anything compared to the thousands of arrests made by the hard-working deputies of the Maricopa County Sheriff's Office were infinitesimal. It was hardly what the media and the crazed Left would have you believe at the time the case was being played out in the media on an almost daily basis.

President Trump and I were always exactly like-minded on immigration, so this wasn't the end of it. With the election of President Trump, we knew the fight would only intensify—and it did.

In 2015, we were brought back into Judge Snow's court for civil contempt charges for claims we were not following his 59-page rules set out for the sheriff's office. The vagueness of the orders made it impossible to comply. He wrongfully assumed we would not continue to carry out our charge to enforce all laws. We were no longer permitted to do saturation raids on employers who were knowingly using illegal aliens in their workforce, nor were we able to raid day labor locations. We weren't, however, kept from stopping vehicles for probable cause or for fighting against human smuggling, gang activity, and other criminal transgressions that would likely ensnare illegal aliens among the perpetrators.

But it was obvious that Judge Snow and the Obama administration didn't want us to cooperate one iota with ICE—ever. At a hearing on the civil contempt charges, I was warned by Snow to get a criminal attorney. The judge was agitated and clearly felt like we investigated him and didn't like the fact that we brought up his wife's restaurant conversation, his alleged bank records from self-proclaimed whistleblower Dennis Montgomery (we never saw these in person), or our attorney's attempt to remove him from the case because of his family conflicts with Covington & Burling.

The entire Snow trial was a miscarriage of justice. Besides Snow's conflict of interest with Covington & Burling, Snow allowed—even insisted—that conversations that I had with the county's previous outside counsel were not protected by attorney-client privilege as the defense put attorney Tim Casey on the stand. Casey refused to absorb any role on the advice (or lack thereof) he provided us on how to comply with Judge Snow's order.

Then, in 2016, several days before early voting was to begin in my sheriff re-election campaign, Judge Snow announced a referral to the U.S. Justice Department for criminal contempt. Certainly, the timing was no accident, as Judge Snow could have made this same erroneous criminal referral months—even years—prior.

The criminal contempt case "landed" in Federal Judge Susan R. Bolton's court. Judge Bolton was a Clinton appointee. She was the judge who heard the federal case against SB 1070 that weakened the law that the citizens of Arizona overwhelmingly supported. Seizing on the opportunity that now presented itself, George Soros poured nearly $3 million into the sheriff's race for my Democratic opponent. As Trump's major ally on illegal immigration law enforcement, I was a very high-profile target. Never before had Soros spent that kind of money on a local election.

Alleged whistleblower Montgomery put together a flow chart showing how the actors in my case were all inter-related and how they connected. This particular witch-hunt could go down as one of the most complicated and politically motivated hoaxes in U.S. history.

Below is a document showing this diagram that shows all the connected parts working against me within the government case. It reads like a similar "who's who" list in the efforts to wreck President Trump, including many of the same actors and co-conspirators.

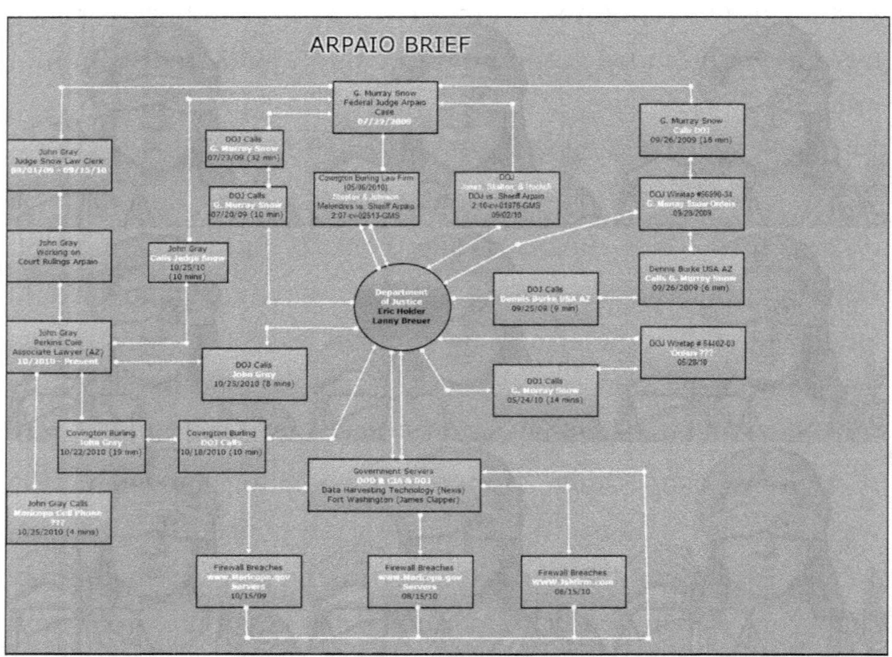

Imagine being a law enforcement professional for more than 55 years, then getting slapped with a criminal prosecution for doing your job! I don't think I've even had two parking tickets in my entire lifetime. Despite the fact that the criminal contempt charges carried the same misdemeanor classification as a citation for a dog owner who couldn't stop his dog barking and disturbing neighbors, it still could carry a six-month sentence.

My attorney continued to fight for a jury trial, guaranteed to each of us as American citizens in our beloved U.S. Constitution, but Bolton would have none of it. She purposely kept the charges at this level, which didn't require a jury trial; however, she could have ruled for a trial by a jury of my peers at any point.

The closing arguments in this case were logical, well-researched and factual. But that had no effect at all, as the outcome was predetermined:

- The government never provided any evidence that I commanded deputies to disobey Snow's order.
- The government never provided any evidence that I interfered with training or compliance of Snow's order.
- My deputies continued to turn people over to ICE and Border Patrol because the order did not clearly and definitively enjoin us from doing so.
- In communicating the order within the Maricopa County Sheriff's Office, attorney Tim Casey readily admitted there was ambiguity in the order.
- Existing case clearly states that, in order for there to exist "criminal contempt" of an order, the order must be clear and definite.

- Every witness presented by the defense indicated the order was ambiguous, and included at least six different interpretations by witnesses from the sheriff's office.
- Even several 9th Circuit Court of Appeals judges had difficulty interpreting the order in practical terms.
- Sheriff deputies continued to act upon instructions from ICE and Border Patrol after the order.
- Arizona state law continued to provide sheriff deputies with the authority to transport an alien, in which confirmation is received from ICE or Border Patrol to federal authorities.
- Sheriff deputies acted on the reasonable belief that he or she was acting as an authorized government agent to assist law enforcement activity.
- The order was never clear on what a deputy was required to do after an illegal alien was encountered during a lawful stop, under federal criminal or state law.

It was apparent that the Justice Department considered *any* stop for an illegal alien, whether it was for cause—or not—to be a violation of an illegal alien's constitutionally protected rights. Since Obama rode to victory partially on a platform of open borders, there is no doubt that me and the Maricopa County Sheriff's Office were going to be front and center in the demonization of enforcing our immigration laws—and that they would label our enforcement actions as racist.

Clearly, spineless politicians began running from any association with the media's slanted coverage on our enforcement operations as racist. It didn't help that even Republicans who had previously sought my endorsement turned on me. This included John McCain and Mitt Romney. Others in the Republican Party would also get their digs in later, when President Trump pardoned me, if they hadn't during the trial. And Senator Jeff Flake, still smarting from the prosecution of his son over animal cruelty charges, was sure to get his comments in.

Others, like Representatives Andy Biggs and Paul Gosar, called it for what it was—a political witch-hunt.

Then, literally days before early voting began, I learned of the guilty verdict from a phone call by my attorney. Judge Bolton didn't even have the decency to have me in court to read the verdict to my face. Perfect timing for the Democrats for the 2016 election! Of course, this was no coincidence or accident. The agenda couldn't have been more obvious.

Immediately, my opponents and the media (many times one and the same) began calling me a "convicted felon." The criminal contempt charge was not a felony; it was a misdemeanor. I sued several national news organizations over their defamation of me as a convicted felon. Some of these cases are still pending.

What really matters here is that President Donald J. Trump knew the facts—and he knew this was a wrongful prosecution. Deep down, President Trump knows I am all about the law. I never came home at night from a long day at the sheriff's office and counted the notches in my belt for how many illegals were arrested that day. My job as a law enforcement officer was to simply enforce the laws we were charged to uphold to the best of my ability—nothing more and nothing less.

Of course, the radicals lost their minds with the pardon, as did some Republicans—so much so that there was a Congressional effort, led by the biased law firm of Perkins Coie, to somehow overturn the pardon and to keep from expunging the verdict. This is not surprising, as those folks aren't typically the kind that study the Constitution. If they were, they'd know a presidential pardon is absolute. We even had to go to the 9th Circuit Court of Appeals to force Judge Bolton to remove the conviction when they rejected our appeal.

There may be a future date awaiting us in the U.S. Supreme Court on that matter!

I can never thank President Trump enough. God bless him.

Chapter 11

The 2018 Arizona Senate Primary

It became obvious to me and most of the country after President Trump was elected that the Left would employ the same tactics used on me (or worse) to undermine this president.

Make no mistake about it: my reason for running in the 2018 Arizona Republican primary was to get elected to Washington, D.C. so I could help President Trump in any way I could. And let's face it, Senator John McCain and Senator Jeff Flake were not Trump supporters. While I respect John McCain's service to our country, he was a vindictive snake when it came to politics. During my first several terms as sheriff, he continually sought my support and endorsement. When I did not support him in the 2000 presidential primary, and instead supported George W. Bush (who, incidentally, won the nomination), McCain was angry with me and neither forgave nor forgot. McCain was like that. If you ever crossed McCain, he would find a way to get you back. President Trump saw this firsthand from him when McCain shot down the congressional overturning of Obamacare.

Flake, on the other hand, was a jelly-spined weasel who was more liberal than conservative. He would never forgive my prosecution of his son and daughter-in-law in the infamous animal cruelty case known as the Green Acres 23. Flake criticized President Trump at every opportunity and became the Left's useful idiot in their attacks on the president.

To be perfectly frank, although I did not have issues with the other two 2018 Arizona senate primary candidates, Kelli Ward and Martha McSally, I really didn't believe either could be of major assistance to President Trump's agenda. Proof of that came in the general election when McSally, who won the primary, lost to ultra-liberal Democrat Kyrsten Sinema.

McSally still made it to the Senate, however, as Republican Governor Doug Ducey appointed her to fill the seat vacated by Senator John Kyl's retirement.

Make no mistake, however; many of the Republicans that supported me in the past refused to endorse me—or worse, would not acknowledge that I was ever in the race. Some even criticized President Trump over the pardon.

I do believe, however, that the heart of the issue of Republican politician support comes down to two very simple things. First, the Obama birth certificate issue, which Republicans dropped like a hot potato, never wanting to explore the obvious facts surrounding the case. Anyone who looked at the factual evidence presented and agreed the birth certificate was a forgery was labeled as a "birther."

For a modern-day politician, a "birther" was akin to being a racist. Somehow, the narrative by the media took hold that someone who believes the birth certificate was not an official document of a half-black president equated to that person being racially motivated.

Second, the racism issue we now see has advanced to the current woke/cancel environment and is to be avoided like the bubonic plague. Republicans and conservatives fear speaking up. One of the reasons I believe President Trump and I have such a great relationship is that we both believe in law and order, including enforcing illegal immigration laws. My law enforcement background with thousands of illegal alien arrests, deportations, Tent City Jails, pink underwear, the restoration of chain gangs, and cooperation with ICE made me a target for being labeled a "racist." And what politician wants to be associated with someone who has been deemed a "racist"? Add the fact that I also get falsely labeled a convicted felon, it's easy to see why weak-spined politicians would think twice about endorsing me, even though I had dozens of national politicians ask for my endorsement on a regular basis in the past.

The 2018 election results were disappointing; I will admit that. The forces against me from the Left and the forces against me in the Republican establishment were too difficult to overcome, just months after a wrongful criminal contempt of court charge and a controversial presidential pardon.

I have no regrets, however, as my goal in running was singular in purpose—to help my hero, President Donald J. Trump, in any way I could.

In June of 2018, a month before the Republican primary in Arizona, my attorneys filed the following report to Attorney General Jeff Sessions. We never received the courtesy of a response.

17851 North 85th Street
Suite 175
Scottsdale, Arizona 85255

Telephone: (480) 626-8483
Facsimile: (480) 502-7500
www.gzlawoffice.com

Mark D. Goldman
mgoldman@gzlawoffice.com

June 1, 2018

Via First Class U.S. Mail, Electronic Mail and Hand Delivery
Honorable Jefferson B. "Jeff" Sessions
Attorney General of the United States
United States Department of Justice
950 Pennsylvania Avenue, N.W.
Washington, D.C. 20530-0001
askdoj@usdoj.gov

Re: Request for Investigation of the Use of Governmental Entities to Influence Elections

Dear Mr. Attorney General:

I represent Joseph Arpaio ("Sheriff Arpaio"), the Sheriff of Maricopa County, Arizona from 1993 until 2017. I respectfully submit this letter on behalf of Sheriff Arpaio.

In 2016, Sheriff Arpaio ran for an unprecedented seventh four-year term. Sheriff Arpaio won the primary in August 2016, but he lost the general election in November 2016. Losing the general election fair and square would not have bothered Sheriff Arpaio. However, that is not what happened. Instead, contrary to its own policies and contrary to the oaths of its leadership and its attorneys, we firmly believe the Department of Justice ("DOJ") pursued a criminal contempt case against Sheriff Arpaio and fed media events coinciding with the primary and general elections for the purpose of ousting him from office. A fair review of the facts as more particularly described here and in the accompanying Memorandum can lead to no other conclusion. Based the conduct of the DOJ and Federal Bureau of Investigation ("FBI") in the criminal prosecution, an investigation is warranted, and that investigation should be handled by an independent special prosecutor or the DOJ's Inspector General.

The requested investigation is all the more warranted because the American public has been and continues to be witnessing daily exposures of activities by the DOJ and FBI

GOLDMAN & ZWILLINGER PLLC

Honorable Jefferson B. "Jeff" Sessions
June 1, 2018
Page 2 of 8

that are just plain shocking, and moreover anathema to the inherent values those institutions are supposed to represent and practice. Therefore, unless and until there is such an investigation, the reputations of the DOJ and FBI will never recover from misconduct that has thus far gone unchecked. Without an investigation and appropriate prosecutions, the misconduct committed with such impunity will spread, with the past, present and future bad actors correctly believing they are immune from accountability and punishment for their misconduct.

For example, two years ago, on August 15, 2016, after President Trump became the republican nominee and candidate for president, as matter-of-factly as though they were ordering a pizza, Peter Strzok, a veteran senior FBI agent, texted to Lisa Page, an attorney for the FBI, the following message:

> I want to believe the path you threw out for consideration in Andy's office [an apparent reference to disgraced and fired Deputy FBI Director Andrew McCabe] that there's no way he gets elected -- but I'm afraid we can't take that risk. It's like an insurance policy in the unlikely event you die before you're 40.

The foregoing is not a quote from an airport kiosk espionage novel. Instead, it is the literal text message between these two FBI employees who were members of Special Counsel Robert Mueller's team investigating President Trump's campaign. To conclude that Strzok and Page were discussing anything other than removing or crippling the future president of the United States of America is delusional. Given that these high-ranking FBI officials had no qualms about discussing methods of overthrowing the future president, it is more than reasonable to believe that the there was a concerted effort to steer and influence the election of Sheriff Arpaio. In other words, it does not take a leap of faith and logic to believe that others at the DOJ and FBI had plans (i.e., "insurance policies") for elections in 2016 other than the presidential election.

The American public elected President Trump in part because they were sick and tired of politics as usual, especially of career politicians on both sides of the aisle and bureaucrats who care about nothing, including having no regard for the rule of law or their oaths, above their jobs, career advancement, re-election and political ambitions. As illustrated in the above quoted Peter Strzok text, these swamp creatures were definitely worried that a President Trump would upend their jobs and careers. The public's call to drain the swamp further militates in favor of the investigation we request in this letter and accompanying Memorandum.

17851 North 85th Street, Suite 175, Scottsdale, Arizona 85255
www.gzlawoffice.com

The Washington elite and the entrenched bureaucrats have and are continuing to use their power to thwart the will of American citizens, who they view with condescension and derisively disregard. This conduct must be immediately investigated, and the culprits discovered, indicted, convicted and punished appropriately. This is not just another power you may choose to exercise, it is an obligation you must meet as Attorney General of the United States. You must investigate this conduct so that it stops and never happens again.

The first question one may ask is "Why have these government officials and institutions engaged in such conduct?" The answer is simple. None of them thought candidate Trump would be elected President, and, consequently, they assumed with a Hillary Clinton lead government, their actions never would have been questioned, let alone investigated and prosecuted. A special counsel must be appointed, or the Inspector General of the DOJ must be empowered to investigate the actions of so called "independent" federal government agencies that have recently engaged in partisan politics, including to the extent they affected or swayed local elections, such as in the 2016 Maricopa County Sheriff election.

Our Republic's existence requires nothing less than a fair and impartial government that focuses on the needs of all Americans, regardless of their political affiliations and regardless of who occupies high positions. It further requires that the public maintain its belief in a fair and impartial system established for the people, by the people. Every citizen must ensure that the federal government remains strong, but, just as important, demand that it also acts within its powers granted by the Constitution. We must fight the drift of the federal government becoming just another corrupt, power-grabbing form of governance like most others in history; we must not allow it to become an oppressive oligarchy generating the type of grievances, misery and suffering that compelled the formation of this great nation. Our representative, constitutional and limited-central-power Republic must stand as formed. Your position serves as a primary guardian against federal overreach and misconduct. We believe that crucial role compels you to act as we request.

Concerns regarding rampant corruption within the FBI and DOJ, as seen leading up to the 2016 presidential election, require a thorough investigation, and prosecutions as deemed appropriate, with full transparency for the public. There is no reasonable disagreement about this. As such, no disagreement can exist about the need for determining how the DOJ weaponized the judicial system in order to interfere with local elections.

Sheriff Joseph Arpaio served as Sheriff of Maricopa County, the fourth most populous county in the nation, for twenty-four years, elected six times by its residents. Sheriff Arpaio survived nearly a quarter century of relentless attacks by the national media,

GOLDMAN & ZWILLINGER PLLC

Honorable Jefferson B. "Jeff" Sessions
June 1, 2018
Page 4 of 8

foreign interests, false-grievance-activists and those who use the misguided among them for their own political purposes, run-of-the-mill political opportunists and, yes, some with heartfelt disputes with his policies and practices. The 2016 election season was different – with additional corrupt people and corrosive acts at play, and it ended in a different result. With the added help of the DOJ, the FBI and the federal courts, Sheriff Arpaio's opponents finally achieved their goals.

In Maricopa County, these players and methods coalesced over a period of years, orbiting around a case seemingly-without-end filed in 2007 and still pending in the United States District Court for the District of Arizona ("District Court"): *Melendres, et al vs. Joseph M. Arpaio, et al.*: Case No. 2:07-cv-2513-GMS ("Melendres case.") Initially filed by community "activists" with the aid of the American Civil Liberties Union, by the Melendres case, Sheriff Arpaio's political opponents first managed to convince the District Court to prevent Sheriff Arpaio from enforcing immigration laws. Soon after, that expanded to a virtual take-over a vast portion of Sheriff Arpaio's elective power and responsibilities. With the election of President Barack Obama ("President Obama") the DOJ intervened and joined in the take-over, lending it the "credibility" and resources of the federal government.

During the 2016 Maricopa County Sheriff's election, Sheriff Arpaio fell victim to the corruption and weaponization of institutions described in this letter and accompanying Memorandum. The DOJ, apparently not satisfied with the prospect of prosecuting a sitting sheriff in federal court, used the judicial system in an effort to defeat Sheriff Arpaio at the ballot box. The DOJ's pattern of announcing charges against Sheriff Arpaio just before crucial dates in the election calendar were designed to oust him from his position by any means necessary. The DOJ's actions, including the timing of their actions, provide no other explanation.

Just days before the August 30, 2016, Arizona GOP primary election, Judge G. Murray Snow, presiding in the Melendres case, issued an order requesting the DOJ to file criminal contempt charges regarding alleged actions occurring over a year and three months prior. This referral launched the new Melendres-case-related criminal case in the United States District Court, referenced above. Setting aside for this letter only the concerns which should immediately arise from the court's unwarranted delay in making the referral, the DOJ must protect its independence when faced with such an order from a judge. Rather than assessing the referral and rejecting it as untimely (if the correct statute had been used, a one year limitation period applied), the DOJ did not. Instead, the DOJ allowed the untimely and improper request to stand and allowed the negative media frenzy to continue through the primary election.

17851 North 85th Street, Suite 175, Scottsdale, Arizona 85255
www.gzlawoffice.com

GOLDMAN & ZWILLINGER PLLC

Failing in its attempts to derail Sheriff Arpaio during the 2016 primary, the DOJ stepped up its politically motivated efforts for the general election. On October 11, 2016, only one day before general election early voting began, the DOJ announced it would file a misdemeanor criminal contempt charge against Sheriff Arpaio. One must suspend all belief and cognitive faculties to conclude that the timing of the actions against Sheriff Arpaio were anything other than political acts and maneuvers.

Empowered by the actions of the DOJ, the order to show cause regarding the contempt charges against Sheriff Arpaio was filed a mere fourteen days before the general election. Worse, the contempt charge was contorted in a way to deny Sheriff Arpaio a jury trial. This means that after about a year and a half from the time the never proven allegations warranting a criminal contempt charge took place, the DOJ and the court it enabled dropped the proverbial hammer on a citizen of the United States, precisely when it would interfere the most with that citizen's legal right to run for public office and precisely when it would most likely mislead and sway voters.

Only a suspension of disbelief allows any conclusion other than under President Obama's leadership, the DOJ engaged in political acts, using the judicial system for the purpose of eliminating Sheriff Arpaio, one of the most prominent and enduring thorns in the side of the now former president and his fellow activists.

Such improper actions were not only used against Sheriff Arpaio. The Inspector General is currently investigating how the DOJ and FBI obtained Foreign Intelligence Surveillance Act ("FISA") warrants against a former Trump campaign aide. Actions were clearly taken to interfere with or sway the 2016 election. Sensitive information indicates that even Sheriff Arpaio's phone may have been tapped, as was brought to the attention of a former FISA Court Judge and provided to FBI officials over two years ago, while the FBI was still under the control of James Comey. To date, no determinations or recommendations have been made, at least publicly, despite the public's right to answers. There is no credible evidence that these improper wiretappings were even investigated by federal authorities.

What is clear is that each step taken by the DOJ in the Melendres case during the 2016 election season produced a flurry of media jubilation and hype, fueling the fire of President Obama and his allies, George Soros and others, granting them a series of gifts for political ads focusing on the DOJ's actions.

While the mere prospect of such corruption is any American patriot's worst fears, exercise of the described political corruption is a living nightmare. Here, the very realistic possibility that the corrupt actors in government may have used the private sector in their

17851 North 85th Street, Suite 175, Scottsdale, Arizona 85255
www.gzlawoffice.com

assault on democracy shudders the very foundation of this great nation. The law firm of Perkins Coie, LLP, which represents the Democratic National Committee, among other politically involved persons or organizations, assisted in the campaign against Sheriff Arpaio, by aiding his opponent directly. Perkins Coie actively engaged in the litigation against Sheriff Arpaio and continues to do so to this day. Perkins Coie has continuously expanded its legal involvement against Sheriff Arpaio, including through the submission of amicus briefs filed in federal court, which are directly adverse to Sheriff Arpaio and its continued efforts to invalidate a legal and proper Presidential pardon. As a reminder, it has been widely reported and acknowledged by Perkins Coie that it hired Fusion GPS during the time in which Fusion GPS obtained the Steele dossier. An investigation is necessary to determine the extent corruption at the DOJ and FBI spread through the use of unaccountable private parties doing their political dirty work. Further, the investigation must determine how such activities were funded.

It is important to further note that the actions of the federal government and Perkins Coie opened the door for the infusion of over three million dollars ($3,000,000) into the campaign against Sheriff Arpaio by political activist George Soros. Soros was able to insert himself in a local political campaign as a result. Soros funded political advertisements that focused on the tens-of-millions of dollars paid by Maricopa County to defend against and then pay for the unelected court-controlled masters, claiming Sheriff Arpaio created the financial burdens on the taxpayers. As such, the very situation supported by Perkins Coie, and made possible by judicial overreach, created a no-win situation for Sheriff Arpaio. Essentially, the judicial system was used by private parties to create chaos by initiating litigation, causing a takeover of a county sheriff's office that cost millions of dollars, then blaming the person under attacked. The use of the judicial system and the federal government to sway local elections must be investigated in order to protect the sanctity of the elections. The electorate has a right to the representation of their choice, not representation produced by manipulation and abuse of power.

The American people have the right to know where corruption in their government exists and how it was allowed to form, fester and thrive with impunity. Logic dictates that there is no reason to believe the partisanship at the FBI stopped with illegally spying on just one of candidate Trump's aides. So, what of the fate of the President's allies, like Sheriff Arpaio, who was systematically attacked on a timeline that proves intent to harm him politically and personally? The public deserves to know the answers to these critical questions. Only you can effectively initiate the processes required to find those answers.

The DOJ's mission statement itself emphasizes the Department's seemingly ignored by many mandate "to ensure fair and impartial administration of justice for all Americans." The Public Integrity Section of the DOJ, in particular, is supposed to root out corruption, not participate in it or act as political witch hunters. The American people have the right to know that government agencies are fair and impartial, no matter which party is in office. The American system depends on this pledge of impartiality. There is good reason and logic behind the rules which forbid the DOJ and other federal officials using the power to influence elections. The Republic must not be weakened by even the impression that improper influence occurred during the 2016 elections.

An investigation will shine light, once and for all, on the obvious corruption within the DOJ and FBI while there is time to reverse the evil trends. If not rooted out now, the rot will spoil much which is unique and good about our nation. When the leaders and employees of the "impartial" agencies which Americans should trust abuse power and play partisan politics, no person, elected or not, is safe from the politically-motivated vendettas recently witnessed. Sheriff Arpaio is not guilty, but most innocent people will not be pardoned by the President, which recently appears to be the only remedy some may have.

The DOJ meddling in the 2016 Maricopa County elections parallel other investigations deemed necessary by your office. You previously ordered the Inspector General to investigate how the DOJ and FBI obtained FISA warrants to spy on Trump aides. The "Nunes Memo", in particular, sheds light on the troubling atmosphere within the federal government that has allowed the stench of underhanded partisanship to spread. The DOJ, in its quest to restore impartiality and regain the trust of the American people, should investigate the extent to which improper politicization played a role in the 2016 Arizona elections and elsewhere.

Based upon the foregoing, and for the reasons described in the accompanying Memorandum, Sheriff Arpaio requests that you appoint a special counsel or direct the Inspector General to investigate the conduct by the DOJ and FBI as they relate to the 2016 Maricopa County Sheriff election and wherever else the facts suggest abuse of power may have occurred. In addition, based on the accompanying Memorandum, Sheriff Arpaio requests that you initiate processes to determine whether the judiciary has unconstitutionally grasped powers not granted to it, or misused existing powers.

Respectfully submitted,

GOLDMAN & ZWILLINGER PLLC

Mark D. Goldman

Mark D. Goldman

17851 North 85th Street, Suite 175, Scottsdale, Arizona 85255
www.gzlawoffice.com

GOLDMAN & ZWILLINGER PLLC

Honorable Jefferson B. "Jeff" Sessions
June 1, 2018
Page 8 of 8

Enclosure: Memorandum in Support

cc: Honorable Charles E. "Chuck" Grassley, Chairman, Senate Committee on the Judiciary
cc: Honorable Robert W "Bob" Goodlatte, Chairman, House of Representatives Judiciary Committee
cc: Honorable Devin Nunes, Chairman, House of Representatives Permanent Select Committee on Intelligence
cc: Mr. Donald F. "Don" McGahn II, White House Counsel

17851 North 85th Street, Suite 175, Scottsdale, Arizona 85255
www.gzlawoffice.com

CHAPTER 12

FINAL THOUGHTS

I've always been an open book—straightforward, transparent and outspoken—in my law enforcement career. Always gung ho to enforce the laws given to me by local, state, and federal authority, I believe in the rule of law and the fair application of those laws to all citizens.

I've locked up drug kingpins, cartel members, gang members, petty criminals, murderers, rapists, thieves, pedophiles, and illegal aliens. My arrests spanned the infamous French Connection as well as politicians and judges. I never really cared what political party any of them identified with or were members of. I am an equal opportunity law enforcement professional—meaning, if people break the law, I will arrest them, no matter who they are.

I had a very successful career in law enforcement before becoming the six-time elected sheriff of Maricopa County. Somewhere in that career, I received the nickname of "America's Toughest Sheriff." I wore that as a badge of honor. The reason for that is that I always related to and felt an incredible duty to the innocent victims of crimes, whether they were children, the elderly, or even animals.

Despite my efforts, I have been fighting an invisible enemy since becoming sheriff. President Trump and I have a common enemy. That enemy is the "Deep State" in the federal government.

I've been fortunate in my career to have met presidents of the United States, presidents and ambassadors of foreign countries, to have lived overseas and traveled the world doing what I love to do, always with Ava at my side.

But I never forget those who depended on me and those who honored me with the courtesy of their vote as their trusted sheriff. I am grateful to Ava and my children for allowing me to live this incredible dream and for a life well-lived.

And the best is yet to come!

Chapter 13

An Epilogue

I'm sure there are some who believe that, because I did not win the 2020 Republican primary for sheriff, I would just ride off into the sunset, relegated to perpetual irrelevancy.

Nothing could be further from the truth. If my enemies think they have heard the last from Sheriff Joe Arpaio, they are sadly mistaken. The media did a thorough job of not covering my campaign for sheriff and, when they did, it was typically a blatant hit piece. My challenge was to make sure voters knew I was running again, so it was totally up to my campaign to get that word out.

During the campaign, I stood in 116-degree heat at various campaign stops all day, every day, taking my message directly to the people. On those days, it was not feasible to wear a mask. Besides, people always wanted pictures of me with the backdrop of President Trump on the beautifully done campaign bus.

Never mind that this campaign was run during the COVID-19 virus, where, at my age of 88 years old, I literally put my life on the line to personally meet and interact with my constituents.

At one point, the pavement got so hot it literally melted the soles off my shoes!

Speaking of age, there is no denying the fact that my age played into the end result. It's also no secret that the local GOP began to abandon me in 2016 as a result of the Melendres trial criminal contempt conviction hoax. Even previously reliant prominent Republicans and local sports team owners, who had always supported my methods, shied away from me in the fall of 2016, and continued to do so in 2018 and 2020.

The two largest issues that caused my fellow Republicans to pause any effort to come out and publicly support me was my unwavering stance on illegal immigration and the infamous alleged Obama birth certificate. Those two topics alone were toxic enough to Republicans who don't share the same conservative courage and, as a result, they shrank like wilted violets, afraid to endorse or support me despite the fact that, behind the scenes, they believed in every step we took to enforce our laws.

In the next phase of my life, I will not be silent—nor will my public support of President Trump waver one iota. I will do everything in my power to help get him re-elected. I know what President Trump has been through, and I've personally felt the same sting suffered by a travesty of justice.

Throughout my career, I've had the backs of rank-and-file law enforcement officers from around the world, and they have had mine. I will always support and fight for the men and women who risk their lives for others on a daily basis. I will never support anti-law enforcement efforts or plans to defund the police, or give in to Marxist anarchists. In the end, America wants law and order. I believe that in every fiber of my being.

Along with attorney Larry Klayman, I will soon be announcing our foundation for fighting crime and corruption, named America's Sheriff, Inc. to represent law enforcement and to protect and preserve the freedoms and liberties conceived of and created on July 4, 1776, by our Founding Fathers.

I have truly led a blessed life, with a great wife and family, the respect of my peers, and the honor of working in law enforcement for 55 years.

I am looking forward to my next unwritten chapter!

Chapter 14

A Few Personal Notes

By David Thomas Roberts

Few times in life does an opportunity present itself to become acquainted with someone whose life experience has been transformational and who has been a hero to many, yet whose intentions and actions are so misunderstood by the average citizen.

When I was presented with the opportunity to meet Sheriff Joe Arpaio, I immediately jumped on a flight from Houston to Phoenix. Sheriff Joe was always a hero to conservatives like me. Tough on crime. Tough on illegal immigration. A consummate law enforcement professional.

When I arrived in Phoenix, my Uber driver got lost and dropped me off at the wrong building, which happened to be the Fountain Hills Chamber of Commerce, in Sheriff Joe's hometown of Fountain Hills, Arizona. Knowing I was in the wrong place, I walked inside anyway and asked the receptionist where I might find Sheriff Joe's office. The receptionist rolled her eyes and pointed me in the right direction. Although she never said anything disparaging about Sheriff Joe, I realized quickly that, for whatever misguided reason, she wasn't a fan of his.

When I finally reached the sheriff's election office, I told him this story, thinking nothing of it. The next day my cell phone rang early in the morning and it was the president of that same local Chamber of Commerce, apologizing to me for her receptionist's attitude and behavior. Later, during the first day I was there but after I left, Sheriff Joe had called her to let her know how her staff treated an out-of-town visitor!

I quickly learned this is prototypical Sheriff Joe Arpaio… Sheriff Joe addresses issues head on, never afraid to ruffle feathers if he believes it is the right thing to do. Never mind that the receptionist was critical in her response about Sheriff Joe; what he was upset about was that was my first contact in his hometown as a visitor from Texas was with someone who was rude and who had an attitude.

During the days, weeks, and months that we worked on this book project, I gained more perspective on Sheriff Joe Arpaio and what makes him tick. There have been several times in my own life where I have been fortunate enough to meet some of my heroes, including Ronald Reagan and Donald Trump. This moment was similar.

Sheriff Joe Arpaio *is* an American Legend. He's John Wayne with a badge. He's a modern-day Wyatt Earp. He is "America's Toughest Sheriff"!

Few people know the danger he was in working undercover in Turkey, or in the United States. On numerous occasions while working for the U.S. Bureau of Narcotics, he was shot at and even kidnapped at one point. As sheriff of Maricopa County, he received 12 credible threats on his life—and he would hunt down each of those individuals, some as far away as Canada, and arrest them. All 12 were eventually convicted. The sheriff had numerous bounties on his head from Mexican drug cartels, the largest being $2 million. An 18-year-old was convicted of a plot to plant a bomb on the sheriff's car, and an Oklahoma man was prosecuted and convicted of mailing an incendiary device to the sheriff's home.

Despite these threats, and unlike so many politicians seen in today's big cities, Sheriff Joe does not carry a gun when out of uniform—and he doesn't have a security detail. He has impressively relied on his gut instincts his entire life—and it has worked for him.

During this amazing process, where I tried to unpack Sheriff Joe's life story, we spent hours upon hours on phone interviews because, shortly after we started, the coronavirus became an issue, locking down travel. Like the peeling of an onion, each layer led to another layer.

It became clear to me very early on that the forces working against Sheriff Joe in many cases were the same forces working—first against candidate Donald Trump, then against him as the president of the United States. It's almost as if the unjust, unethical, and criminal political witch-hunt that tagged Sheriff Joe with criminal contempt was a dry run for President Trump.

Peeling back the layers of the actors in the attempted destruction of Sheriff Joe Arpaio are the same actors in the news today, attempting to do the same to President Trump. If you set up a criminal case board on the wall tracking the political and criminal hit job on Sheriff Joe, you would see names linked by direct lines and dotted lines to bad actors like former FBI Director James Comey, former Attorney General Eric Holder, George Soros, the law firms of Covington & Burling and Perkins Coie (Steele Dossier, Fusion GPS, etc.), John Brennan, Loretta Lynch, and the good guys like General Flynn and Roger Stone.

The Left's incessant and consistent coordinated efforts to marginalize and defeat Sheriff Joe Arpaio are also a direct attack on President Trump. Sheriff Joe makes no apologies in unequivocally stating that he's only had one hero in his life, and it's President Donald Trump.

To be frank, I feel they are very similar in personalities and beliefs, although I've obviously spent much more time with the sheriff. The most common trait? The are both "counter-punchers" and have a knack for getting to the root of an issue, even if it exposes a nerve.

There is no doubt in my mind that Sheriff Joe touched on the nerve that would ultimately motivate his opponents to pull out all stops to defeat him and ultimately try to silence him, and it continues to this day. And, although the arrests and deportations of thousands of illegal aliens, the Tent City Jails, the pink underwear, and the chain gangs were controversial because the Left made them controversial, there is no doubt where the magnitude of the Left's collective losing of their mind emanates from...

The fake Obama birth certificate. *Period.*

The fact that a local sheriff would take on this investigation should shed much light on who Sheriff Joe really is. He has said countless times to me that, when it comes to enforcing the law, he doesn't care who it is. Spurred by the requests from his constituents about the validity of a presidential candidate in his county, the sheriff worked to "exonerate" President Obama and put this to bed once and for all.

When it became obvious that the birth certificate was, in fact, a forgery, his entire life changed.

And, make no mistake about it, everything that has happened to Sheriff Joe involving his issues with the Justice Department and federal judges stems from the fact that the sheriff was only doing his job on this issue.

To be frank, an entire book and documentary could be done on this investigation alone, and the twists and turns of the plots, with an alleged NSA whistleblower and very prominent and highly placed government officials involved, would read like one of the most fascinating suspense novels of all time. But it isn't a novel; Sheriff Joe actually lived it.

It has been one of the highlights of my literary and professional career to have worked on this project.

Not only is Sheriff Joe Arpaio a legend, he's an American treasure.

BOY SCOUTS OF AMERICA

THE SILVER BEAVER AWARD

FOR DISTINGUISHED SERVICE TO YOUTH

Presented to

Joseph M. Arpaio

Upon nomination by the

Grand Canyon Council

and with the approval of the National Court of Honor
The officers of the National Council of the Boy Scouts of America hereby affix their signatures and the corporate seal.

February 10, 2000

PRESIDENT

CHAIRMAN NATIONAL COURT OF HONOR

NATIONAL COMMISSIONER

CHIEF SCOUT EXECUTIVE

BOY SCOUTS OF AMERICA

BE PREPARED

Sheriff Joe receives Boy Scouts of America Award

Sheriff Joe with Franklin Graham

Sheriff Arpaio with Ben Carson

Sheriff Joe with Jane Seymour

Sheriff Joe with Jon Voight

Sheriff Joe and his wife Ava with Lee Greenwood

Sheriff Joe with Charles Barkley

Sheriff Joe with Steven Seagal

Sheriff Joe with Glen Campbell

Sheriff Joe with Mike Tyson

Sheriff Joe with Dwayne Johnson, "The Rock"

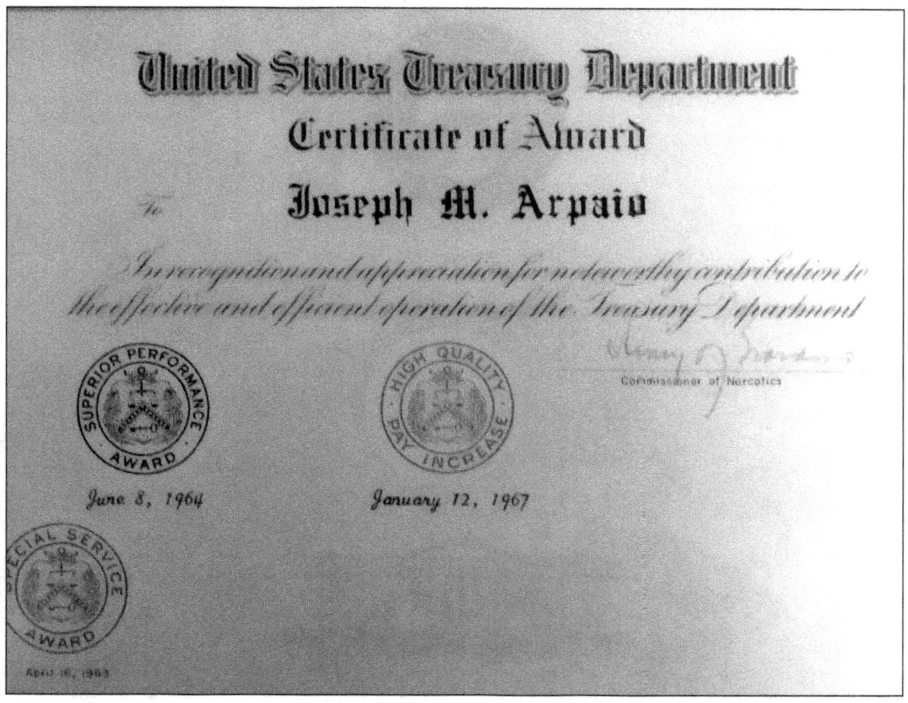

United States Treasury Department

Certificate of Award

To Joseph M. Arpaio

In recognition and appreciation for noteworthy contribution to the effective and efficient operation of the Treasury Department

Commissioner of Narcotics

SUPERIOR PERFORMANCE AWARD

June 8, 1964

HIGH QUALITY PAY INCREASE

January 12, 1967

SPECIAL SERVICE AWARD

Joe Arpaio receives United States Treasury Department Award

Sheriff Joe at Veterans Parade

Award for Outstanding Sheriff

Scottsdale Masonic Lodge # 43
On this twenty-fourth day of October, 2013
Hereby recognizes Maricopa County Sheriff,
Sheriff Joe Arpaio
For his outstanding performance to uphold his duty, to the people of this County, State and his Country

H. Ritchie Jordan
Secretary

Worshipful Master

Sheriff Joe receives Outstanding Sheriff Award

About America's Toughest Sheriff

Joseph M. Arpaio

Professional Experience

March 1954-June 1957	Police Officer Metropolitan Police Department Washington, DC
June 1957-Nov. 1957	Police Officer Las Vegas Police Department Las Vegas, NV
Nov. 1957-Oct. 1961	Special Agent U.S. Bureau of Narcotics Chicago, IL
Oct. 1961-Oct. 1964	Special Agent in Charge U.S. Bureau of Narcotics Istanbul, Turkey
Oct. 1964-Jan. 1967	Special Agent in Charge U.S. Bureau of Narcotics San Antonio, TX

Jan. 1967-Aug. 1968	Special Agent in Charge U.S. Bureau of Narcotics U.S. Treasury Department Washington, DC Field Office
Aug. 1968-Dec. 1968	Deputy Regional Director U.S. Bureau of Narcotics & Dangerous Drugs Baltimore, Maryland Region
Jan.1970-July 1973	Regional Director Mexico City (Mexico, Central and South America) U.S. Bureau of Narcotics & Dangerous Drugs Department of Justice
July 1973-July 1974	Section Chief Office of Intelligence U.S. Drug Enforcement Administration Washington, DC
Aug. 1974-July 1978	Deputy Regional Director U.S. Drug Enforcement Administration Boston, Massachusetts Region
July 1978-July 1982	Special Agent in Charge of Arizona U.S. Drug Enforcement Administration
Jan. 1993-Dec. 2016	Sheriff Maricopa County, Arizona

Military Service

1950-1953	U.S. Regular Army, Sergeant
1954-1964	U.S. Army, Warrant Officer Criminal Investigation Division (Reserves)

Education

	Attended University of Maryland
Oct. 1953-Jan. 1954	New York Institution of Criminology
1958	Federal Bureau of Narcotics Training School
July 1961	U.S. Treasury Department Technical Investigative School
May 1969	U.S. Civil Service Commission Executive Seminar Kings Point, Long Island, New York, NY
June 1971	American Management Association New York, NY
June 1974	American Management Association
October 1975	U.S. Attorney General's Senior Executive Seminar FBI Academy Quantico, Virginia
Mar. 1976	U.S. Civil Service Commission (Labor Relations & Collective Bargaining)
Jan. 1977	U.S. Deputy Attorney General's Public Policy Seminar Washington, DC

Numerous other classes, seminars, workshops and conferences sponsored by educational or professional institutions.

Awards & Citations

1963-1964, 1967	Numerous Superior Performance Awards U.S. Treasury Department
1964	Exceptional Service Award from General Director Turkish National Police

1968	Extraordinary Service Award Office of Special Investigations U.S. Air Force Washington, DC
	Award from San Antonio, Texas Police Department
	Letter of Commendation U.S. Attorney General Washington, DC
	Special Service Award U.S. Bureau of Narcotics & Dangerous Drugs
1969	Award from Baltimore, Maryland Police Department
1971	Award from Mexico's Attorney General, Mexico City
1972	Letter of Commendation U.S. Attorney General Washington, DC
	Award from Baltimore, Maryland Police Department
1973	Letter of Commendation U.S. Ambassador to Mexico
1978	Excellence of Performance Award U.S. Drug Enforcement Administration Department of Justice
1980	Sustained Superior Performance Award U.S. Drug Enforcement Administration Department of Justice
1981	Outstanding Contribution in the Field of Narcotics International Narcotic Enforcement

	Officers Association Minneapolis, MN
1982	Award from Arizona Association Chiefs of Police
	Special Award of Honor from International Narcotics Association
2000	Silver Beaver Award, Arizona Boy Scouts Council for Distinguished Service to the Youth
	Anslinger Award for Counterdrug Activity International Narcotic Enforcement Officers Association
2003	Outstanding Italian-American for Arizona, Sons of Italy
2007	National Humanitarian Award American Humane Society
2008	Sheriff Buford Pusser "Walking Tall" National Law Enforcement Officer of the Year
2014	American Hall of Fame
	National Award Recognition Sheriff of the Year, We Trip
	Hero of Freedom Award Western Center for Journalism
2015	Americanism Civis-Illustris Award for Enhancing Public Welfare presented by UNICO
	Longest-serving Sheriff, Maricopa County (24 years), recognized by Arizona State Historian Marshall Timble

As sheriff from 1993-2016 has been featured and profiled thousands of times by worldwide news media (newspapers, magazines, radio and television), and recipient of numerous international, national, and local awards and citations.

Affiliations

Member	Arizona Association of Chiefs of Police The American Legion National Italian-American Foundation
Life Member	International Association of Chiefs of Police National Sheriffs' Association
Past Pres/Life Member	International Narcotic Enforcement Officers' Association
Charter Member	Association of Former Federal Narcotics Agents
Commissioner	Governor's Arizona Criminal Justice Commissions

Personal Data

Born June 14, 1932 (Springfield, Massachusetts)

Married 62 years, two children, four grandchildren.

www.ingramcontent.com/pod-product-compliance
Lightning Source LLC
LaVergne TN
LVHW010058110826
845155LV00028B/401
* 9 7 8 1 9 4 8 0 3 5 9 5 8 *